INVASION (

Praise for

It was only a matter of time before a clever publisher realized that there is an audience for whom *Exile on Main Street* or *Electric Ladyland* are as significant and worthy of study as *The Catcher in the Rye* or *Middlemarch* … The series … is freewheeling and eclectic, ranging from minute rock-geek analysis to idiosyncratic personal celebration
— *The New York Times Book Review*

Ideal for the rock geek who thinks liner notes just aren't enough
— *Rolling Stone*

One of the coolest publishing imprints on the planet
— *Bookslut*

These are for the insane collectors out there who appreciate fantastic design, well-executed thinking, and things that make your house look cool. Each volume in this series takes a seminal album and breaks it down in startling minutiae. We love these. We are huge nerds
— *Vice*

A brilliant series … each one a work of real love
— *NME* (UK)

Passionate, obsessive, and smart
— *Nylon*

Religious tracts for the rock 'n' roll faithful
— *Boldtype*

[A] consistently excellent series
— *Uncut* (UK)

We … aren't naive enough to think that we're your only source for reading about music (but if we had our way … watch out). For those of you who really like to know everything there is to know about an album, you'd do well to check out Bloomsbury's "33 1/3" series of books
— *Pitchfork*

For almost 20 years, the 33-and-a-Third series of music books has focused on individual albums by acts well known (Bob Dylan, Nirvana, Abba, Radiohead),cultish (Neutral Milk Hotel, Throbbing Gristle, Wire) and many levels in-between. The range of music and their creators defines "eclectic," while the writing veers from freewheeling to acutely insightful. In essence, the books are for the music fan who (as Rolling Stone noted) "thinks liner notes just aren't enough."
—*The Irish Times*

For reviews of individual titles in the series, please visit our blog at 333sound.com and our website at https://www.bloomsbury.com/academic/music-sound-studies/

Follow us on Twitter: @333books

Like us on Facebook: https://www.facebook.com/33.3books

For a complete list of books in this series, see the back of this book.

Forthcoming in the series:

Invasion of Privacy

Ma'Chell Duma

BLOOMSBURY ACADEMIC
NEW YORK · LONDON · OXFORD · NEW DELHI · SYDNEY

BLOOMSBURY ACADEMIC
Bloomsbury Publishing Inc
1385 Broadway, New York, NY 10018, USA
50 Bedford Square, London, WC1B 3DP, UK
29 Earlsfort Terrace, Dublin 2, Ireland

BLOOMSBURY, BLOOMSBURY ACADEMIC and the
Diana logo are trademarks of Bloomsbury Publishing Plc

First published in the United States of America 2024

Library of Congress Cataloging-in-Publication Data
Names: Duma, Ma'Chell M., author.
Title: Invasion of privacy / Ma'Chell M. Duma.
Description: [1.] | New York : Bloomsbury Academic, 2024. |
Series: 33 1/3 | Includes bibliographical references. |
Summary: "Explores the record smashing, critically adored, 2018 debut of
Bronx rapper Cardi B, that kicked a Louboutin through Hip Hop misogyny to
become one of the most successful debuts of all time"– Provided by publisher.
Identifiers: LCCN 2023034124 (print) | LCCN 2023034125 (ebook) |
ISBN 9781501389276 (paperback) | ISBN 9781501389283 (epub) |
ISBN 9781501389290 (pdf) | ISBN 9781501389306
Subjects: LCSH: Cardi B, 1992-. Invasion of privacy. | Rap (Music)–United States–
History and criticism. | Popular music–United States–2011-2020–History
and criticism. | Women rap musicians. | Sex in music.
Classification: LCC ML420.C2546 D85 2024 (print) |
LCC ML420.C2546 (ebook) | DDC 782.421649092–dc23/eng/20230823
LC record available at https://lccn.loc.gov/2023034124
LC ebook record available at https://lccn.loc.gov/2023034125

ISBN: PB: 978-1-5013-8927-6
           ePDF: 978-1-5013-8929-0
           eBook: 978-1-5013-8928-3

Series: 33 1/3

Typeset by Integra Software Services Pvt. Ltd.
Printed and bound in Great Britain

To find out more about our authors and books visit www.bloomsbury.com and sign up for
our newsletters.

To Strummer

The very best kid a mom who blasts "WAP" could ask for.

Contents

CONTENTS

Acknowledgments

Thank you to Shawty Astrology, Sara Bennett, Erik Blood, Rachel Crain, Tricia Diamond, Aaron and Emily Duma, Ty Duma, Ted and Mary Duma, Rachael Ferguson, Corey Gutch, the LaVassar family, Ariana LaBarrie, Angele Moyseos, Frank Nieto, Sara E. Pina, Ebony Purks, Ben Verellen (and everyone at Bar House), Natalie Zina Walschots, and Seattle's very potent sativa strains and coffee. You all helped make this book possible.

I'd like to also acknowledge the work of Ariana LaBarrie*, who handled the boring administrative tasks (for which she was wayyyyy over qualified) associated with this book like a boss.

*Ariana LaBarrie is a content creator specializing in pop culture from Detroit, MI. The founder of the entertainment website fresh pair of iis, she holds a B.A. from the University of Michigan, a M.A. from NYU and a M.S. from Northwestern University. Her favorite Cardi B verse is "No Limit."

Foreword

In my opinion the best *33 ⅓* makes a person who has never heard the album understand what it's about, why it's important, and have as good an understanding of what it sounds like as can be described on paper. I'm so honored to be the one who gets to do it for this particular record.

I love *Invasion of Privacy*.

All music fans have a record that saves them at a moment when they needed it most and Cardi's debut is mine.

It is also a record in a genre that is not mine, culturally.

To address this throughout the writing of this book I've paid younger writers of color for their administrative time on the project and offered to mentor them through their own submission process to the series. This does not make me some sort of civil rights genius. My consciousness about this effort is due to the fact I, as everyone occasionally is, a jackass, making tons of mistakes in the past that you try and learn from, to the only real apology is not repeating your actions.

I've tried really hard to understand what my lane was here and stay in it.

I'm hoping our equity model is one that will be beneficial but I'm sure, and hope, within a few years, it will seem antiquated. The book's equitization is modeled after the brilliant work of Natasha Marin, whose *Reparations Project* asks people who benefit from color privilege to do something within their grasp and means to make equitable change. The idea is that no one person can undo systemic racism themselves through a single act but by collective achievable acts we can make progress.

You'll find through the course of the book mentions of other work by Black women on the subjects addressed here. Please seek their titles out.

I've also tried to back up my own opinion with published work by authors of color whenever possible. This is by no means all the work out there but maybe a starter kit to learn more.

Given the limited word count (famously 33,333) I can only touch on subjects that themselves deserve their own books.

I've also tried to cite all possible sources in the footnotes so credit is given and the original works can be explored.

That being said, please enjoy your read. I hope you are as entertained as you are informed and that the book does as right by Cardi, as she has done by me.

Ma'Chell Duma

Introduction of Terms

Through the course of this book I'll be frequently referring to terms you may not have heard before or can be used in multiple contexts or have historically evolved.

I've listed a few below. I hope it serves as a guide to how I'll be using language going forward.

Femme—Borrowing from Lesbian culture, Femme is used to denote characteristics we associate with traditional femininity. Because femme-ness is not specific to a gender but an overall characteristic, I use femme as a term to encompass female identifying people making Rap. Femme, female, and woman or women will be used interchangeably, in a broad and encompassing way, in front of "rapper" throughout the reading, especially in the work of others.

Pussy Rap—A genre of Rap best defined by what we'll call the "Pull Over" equation. Most will cite Lil' Kim as the Godmother of the genre and that's true, but it's Trina's "Pull Over" that clearly denotes all the characteristics of contemporary Pussy Rap.[1] Not every person with a vagina who raps makes Pussy

[1]See Chapter 3, "Bickenhead."

Rap. Technically, if you follow the Trina equation, someone with xy chromosomes could make Pussy Rap; Saucy Santana, a femme gay man, makes Pussy Rap.

Feminism—Cardi's definition of feminism is simply "equity" and she is correct.[2] When I refer to feminism in the book, it is referring to the feminist principle of intersectional equity. The Webster's definition "belief in and advocacy of the political, economic, and social equality of the sexes expressed especially through organized activity on behalf of women's rights and interests"[3] is also accurate in the book's context.

Matriarchy—For the book we'll be using matriarchy in the broader context as "Institutions where women make the principal decisions." Webster's defines a matriarch as a woman who rules or dominates a family, group, or state.[4]

Patriarchy—Webster's has a technical "broad" definition for patriarchy as "control by men of a disproportionately large share of power" and it accurately matched how it will be used in the course of reading.

And … I'm not going to be using the N word in this book. When I refer to "undistinguished gentlemen," we all know what I mean. I'm also not going to police Black folks' speech, so all quotes from POC will be kept intact.

[2]73 Questions with Cardi B | *Vogue*
[3]https://www.merriam-webster.com/dictionary/feminism
[4]https://www.merriam-webster.com/dictionary/matriarch

Introduction

Let me Fat in Peace
—Cardi B., Twitter

There is much to be admired in the creation of a baroque porcelain corset.

First comes a painstakingly customized form—cut from fabric or leather, made to fit its wearer like a second skin. The intricate pattern is then recreated with custom fired, individual glass pieces that comprise the garment.

The artist begins delicate application of flaked gold leaf set to shimmer on the corset's boning, and applies the first of what will become layers upon layers of hardening lacquer.

Then, piece by piece, ornate, handmade fluers are secured to the form, glided, and lacquered again.

Next comes the micro-detailed hand painting to create swirls of delicate florals in muted pastels, each executed with pinpoint precision, after which another coat of lacquer is applied.

With a jeweler's loupe, so the details can be magnified to the bare eye, gems are then placed one by one on the garment with a tweezer fine enough to pick up a single silk thread. Once interlaced in the seam, the jewels are encrusted in more lacquer.

The process continues till the garment has fully formed.

While the lacquer, classically made from tree resins, maybe the least valuable material in what composes this piece of wearable art, is by far its most important element. Fine and fragile, the glass and ornate decoration are merely beautiful on their own.

It's the lacquer that binds the corset's strength.

And its resilience.

And ultimately, its shine.

The result of those layers upon layers upon layers of lacquer and precious materials is glamorous armor, meant to highlight all the most feminine aspects of the form it adorns, as at home in the bedroom as it would be on the battlefield.

While such audacious attire could have been crafted for Catherine the Great, the habiliment described above was created for another queen from a land once referred to as the Manor of Morrisania, Belcalis Marlenis Almánzar.

Lady Almánzar was not born royalty. Her ascension was earned. She is best known not by her given name, but as the custom-crafted, precisely painted, bejeweled in diamonds and gold persona she formed for herself.

The process is not at all unfamiliar to a girl from what we now know as the Bronx, as the method one uses to create a porcelain corset is remarkably similar to one used to create the preferred artful weaponry of the contemporary, urban warrior—the acrylic nail.

Her "Lacquer" comes in the form of life lessons. Each stumble on her journey from poor South Bronx kid to *Fame*-style performing arts high schooler to stripper to social media personality to reality star, culminating in her ascension to a household name—whose number one debut album, *Invasion of Privacy*, would become one of the most critically and commercially successful records of the new millennia, each adding another fortifying layer of depth and strength to the fantastical, shining creation that is Cardi B.

In the custom corset by the Netherlands-based artist Joyce Spackman—whose creations use modern thermoplastic in place of traditional porcelain and its accompanying bikini bottom, leg, arm, and hand pieces—Cardi is clad in little else. The creation is accompanied by a filmy, nude body stocking and her signature three-inch, sky blue, heavily jeweled, acrylics modeled after the sets made famous by her personal nail designer Jenny Bui.

With the efforts of her glam squad, Cardi is a hyper-sexed Botticelli's Venus, in all her exaggerated, flowing, ultra-blonde glory. She is accompanied by scantily clad nymphets and fittingly showcasing a coveted Vush—Your Majesty 2, premium vibrator. It's just one of several, outrageously artful looks the "Up" video will showcase, but stands out as stunningly memorable, each detail as meticulously crafted as the last, right down to the corset's gold ornamentation recreated on her six-inch, Lucite, stripper-favored high heel.

As she emerges from her porno half-shell on the set of the video for "Up" Cardi is on top. She is *Billboard*'s 2020 Woman of the Year. She holds five *Guinness World Records*; has appeared on *Time* magazine's list of the 100 Most Influential

People; her debut is on course to be the longest charting record by a female rapper in history; she is the first woman to win a Grammy for Best Rap Album, and the female rapper with the most billion "streamers" on Spotify. She is also the first person of Dominican descent to top the *Billboard* 200 in its fifty plus-year history.

To say Cardi had cemented her place as a dominant force in pop culture is an understatement; with a reach extending beyond entertainment, serious journalists saw her commandeer interviews with the top two Democratic candidates for president of the United States in the 2020 election cycle.

It's her debut on Atlantic Records, 2018's *Invasion of Privacy* that has served as the catalyst to this stratospheric launch. Multi-platinum and commanding a spot on the *Billboard 200* for three consecutive years, *Invasion of Privacy*'s thirteen tracks are at times pure Rap bravado, at times intimately confessional, and always intent on female pleasure and power, making her the model for the new "female rapper."

Whereas some artists find gender qualifiers negate their accomplishments, Cardi takes a different approach embracing the title of "Female Rapper," telling *XXL*'s Vanessa Satten:

> So, I feel like it's so amazing to be a woman. I don't give a fuck if somebody call me a female rapper. A female entrepreneur. A female this. That's what I am.
>
> Like, I'm a whole female and I'm winning awards on niggas. And I'm making numbers on you niggas. I have

a song on my album and I'd say, "Y'all niggas ain't doing the numbers that my last shit did." And I really could've said, "Y'all bitches ain't doing the numbers that my last shit did." But it was like, not even y'all muthafuckas is doing my numbers. So, it's just like, I don't give a fuck. Yes, I am a girl. With a pussy. With titties. And it's just like, "Oh my God, she's so pretty, but she's so smart. She's such a killa." I just feel so powerful being a girl that I don't give a damn if you call me a female rapper or a female … Yes, I am a girl.[1]

*****

"What's poppin' *Saturday Night Live*? We sinnin' tonight, and we going to church tomorrow, Hallelujah!" exalted a triumphant Cardi B during her first performance of the evening, an orchestrated remixed melody of "Bodak Yellow" and "Bartier Cardi" performed in Spanish and English.

A *Saturday Night Live* musical guest slot has historically proved a pivotal launching point for young artists, but as *Invasion of Privacy* had debuted at number one the day prior, it made Cardi's performance more of a victorious celebration. April 2018 will be a fantastic month for the rapper with her #1 album drop placing her among the seminal ranks of Lauryn Hill's *The Miseducation of Lauryn Hill* in Hip-Hop history.[2]

---

[1] *XXL* magazine, Spring, 2021.
[2] Upon its three-year anniversary in 2021, *Invasion of Privacy* was still in the *Billboard* Hot 200 making it the longest charting album from a female rapper in history.

With all the zeal of a hometown girl making good, she took the stage with four dancers in an outfit that paid tribute to the fingerwaves of Josephine Baker, the black and white villainesse sheik of Cruella DeVille, and the technicolor fresh outrageousness of her rap mentor Missy Elliott—inspired by, but not identical to the look on the *Invasion of Privacy* cover. The ensemble's black and white feathered skirt, architectural and oversized, was not only a fashion statement but a clever concealment device.

Cardi used her second performance of the night not only to debut a live version of the single "Be Careful"—a powerful ballad about doing a bad girl, gone good, wrong, to blow up the internet. Speculation about a possible "bun in the oven" had created a digital fever where Cardi cheekily replied to her army of Twitter followers (or Bardi Gang, as they call themselves) after an inquiry: "Bitch, I'm just getting fat. Let me fat in peace."[3]

Starting the performance with the camera and spotlight close, it was subtly drawn out during the performance's midsection, the light settling on and illuminating the midsection of her white bodycon Christian Siriano dress, and its well-developed, baby bump. The crowd unleashed a roar and Queen Belcalis from the Bronx dropped another publicity bomb on social media.

Her fam, fans, and foes would expect nothing less.

[3]*Complex* magazine, Feb. 4, 2018.

1

Get Up Ten

> Cardi B suggests a new lane for female rappers—one
> that has little to do with seeking permission from male
> gatekeepers, pandering to white culture, or criticizing
> other women for their sexuality. It is about finding
> an audience on your own terms.[1]
> —Kristin Corry, *Pitchfork*

In 1984 Vanessa Williams, the first Black Miss America, was
forced to renounce her crown when nude photos she'd taken as a
young model were published by *Penthouse*. The arty, high gloss,
softcore shots would hardly constitute "porn" by 2020 standards,
but Williams spent much of the remainder of the 1980s
recultivating her image. Williams's return to entertainment and
ongoing success across a variety of fields (she was issued a public
apology by the Miss America Pageant in 2015[2]) is a comeback
story the stuff of which Cardi's "Get Up Ten" is made.

---

[1]https://pitchfork.com/thepitch/why-cardi-bs-bodak-yellow-no-1-matters/
[2]Roberts, Robin. "Vanessa Williams on Returning to Miss America after
Scandal." *ABC News*. Retrieved Sept. 11, 2015.

The public shaming Williams received strikes a broad contrast to the treatment Madonna[3] received when a year later she was faced with a similar scandal.

It should come as no surprise that a white artist already working in popular music, a morally grayer medium and whose art was already deemed overtly sexual, was given a quicker rehabilitation and the privilege of shrugging off the incident with a "so what?"

Generations of women in entertainment have engaged in forms of sex work prior to success, few have been able to be open about it.

Cardi's apt ability to navigate reality TV and social media may have brought her to the public's consciousness, but her savvy was honed prior to Vine or Instagram, with the aforementioned traits cultivated early in her time working as a stripper and her subsequent refusal to be shamed for the work—an action that in itself opens the door for women to support and pay for their art within the spectrum of sex work that was not possible before.

The Yale Global Health Justice Partnership in Partnership with Sex Workers and Allies Network defines sex work as:

> Sex work, broadly defined, is the exchange of sexual services for money or goods, including housing, food, drugs, or basic necessities. It may involve working independently, with others, or for a third party. Individuals may engage in sex work regularly or sporadically. Sex workers include people of all genders, races, and ages. Some forms of sex work (the exchange of sexual conduct

[3]*Playboy,* Sept., 1985.

for money or goods) are prohibited by prostitution laws, while other kinds, such as stripping or erotic dancing, are regulated by laws such as zoning or alcohol laws, and are not criminal, per se.

Work in the sex sector/sex trades occurs in many different forms and settings, including street-based or web-based settings, escort services, and video camera work, among others … However, while the term was adopted by persons within the sex trades as a self-designation, not everyone who participates in the sex trades identifies as a sex worker.[4]

Prior to the release of *Invasion of Privacy*, in an interview with *The Guardian*, Cardi addressed the topic:

"Would people feel some type of way if I was a cashier-turned-rapper?" she asks today, weary of how the ex-stripper tag is disproportionately used to define her. "People want me to be so full of shame that I used to dance. I would never be ashamed of it. I made a lot of money, I had a good time and it showed me a lot—it made me open my eyes about how people are, how men are, about hunger, passion and ambition."[5]

She told *Cosmopolitan* the vocalization of her time on the pole was to help create more respect for women who dance:

"People say, 'Why do you always got to say that you used to be a stripper? We get it.' Because y'all don't respect me because of it, and y'all going to respect these strippers from

[4]Issue Brief: Sex Work vs Trafficking *(yale.edu)*.
[5]*The Guardian*, Dec. 1, 2017.

now on … Just because somebody was a stripper don't mean they don't have no brain."[6]

She uses stripping, and the backlash, to launch *Invasion of Privacy*.

On the very first verse of the very first track, "Get Up Ten" and she comes at it spitting fire. Sampled emergency sirens wane against juxtaposed twinkling piano keys, declaring with urgency that she was given two options—"stripping or lose," snapping the listener to attention. This juxtaposition is pure Cardi—feminine and forceful. She then goes on to drop the detail that the club where she danced was across from her school, a line meant to not just spill the tea but knock the table over.

Before you can put the ass in assumption, she commands the narrative again, stating she was there to dance, not have sex, and that there is a difference, thank you. The result is a stand out track that cements its status as one of Rap's great origin stories.

The track's stark opening lets Cardi assert her position first and foremost as a rapper. She is telling her story, the record is being set, and your input is irrelevant. As her profile as a pop culture figure and entertainer flourished, she let you know from the jump she didn't need flashy production, a recognizable sample, or even a beat to follow to prove her prowess.

The Hip-Hop podcast *No Skips* devoted to flawless Rap records likened "Get Up Ten" to the warning shots you fire when holding up a bank, meant to draw your attention and hold it till she is good and ready to dismiss you, forcing you

---

[6]https://www.cosmopolitan.com/entertainment/a18210415/cardi-b-april-cover/

to note her lyrical daring, and challenging her detractors to "shut up or shoot her."[7]

"Get Up Ten" is 3:51 minutes that pulls you in and makes you root for her for the rest of the record's remaining 44. For over a minute and 20 seconds Cardi holds the beat with just her phrasing paced by short piano notes, her flow driving the track's slowly increasing tempo topping out at 93 bpms. The minimalism is a stroke of genius, letting us focus on her lyrics and expert delivery, daring the listener to drop their attention. The track, helmed by producers DJ SWANQ and Matt Allen, progressively builds around the 2:05 mark into a shimmering layer cake of sound with instrumentation and samples building on each other—the bass throbs, the opening keys and sirens reappear, shotguns load and discharge and her vocals sit high in front of the mix still leading the auditory charge.

Controlling her own narrative defines Cardi's earliest work. On the mix tapes where she honed her craft, *Gansta Bitch Music (Volume 1 & 2)*, she frequents the topic, her first, self-released single bluntly titled "Stripper Ho."

Much like "Stripper Ho," "Get Up Ten" is meant to take ownership of her own story but goes deeper, both lyrically and melodically. "Stipper Ho" is hooky fun with winky jokes and clever lyrics. The video for "Stripper Ho" sees her invoke Deebo from *Friday*, but she only needs her fineness to walk down the street and take everything you have.

"Get Up Ten" seeks its truth in the autobiographical. It's smarter. It's darker. It's subversively funnier. It shows her growth as an artist and storyteller, taking ownership of the

---

[7] *No Skips with Jinx & Shea*, Vol. 2, Ep. 2, Cardi B. *Invasion of Privacy*.

"stripper" narrative male rappers had been proliferating since Hip-Hop's inception to the point where "Strip Club Rap" or rap about strippers is its own sub-genre.

Strip Club Rap rarely centers the dancer in the narrative and when it does it is often done from a point of victimhood. When Cardi says she could strip or be average—which to her constitutes a loss—she denotes a clear choice. She is not a victim. She is clear about her circumstances and would rather not be a cashier. And while many women do dance to support family or overcome circumstances some would deem stereotypical, Cardi doesn't draw the line between herself and those women, only between those who are engaging in prostitution, as they are two distinctly different things. It's noticeably different from when her male counterparts solely hold the pen.

Music about strippers was not historically confined to a specific genre, however. The L.A. 1980s hair metal scene was funded by women who danced on the Sunset Strip that happened to share an address with some of the city's most legendary music venues. Members of Guns N' Roses, Poison, and various bands of the era acknowledge that strippers were paying for their housing, Aqua Net hairspray, drugs, and basic survival. Like rock 'n' roll Robin Hoods they took from rich, Los Angeles yuppie squares and gave to these glammy, broke boys brokering art and commerce as both muse and patron.

The 1990s saw the start of conversations around the intersection of sex work and art and commerce intersecting with mainstream music and pop culture. Both Bikini Kill's Kathleen Hanna and Hole's Courtney Love worked as strippers to fund their bands in the 1990s and spent much of their time supporting their subsequent records being interrogated about the issue by male DJs and music writers.

Both Love and Hanna were members of a music-centric third wave of white feminism. They remained outliers when it came to openly discussing dancing as part of their past, but they were able to establish the first tiny cracks in the stigmas Cardi would later smash.

The rise of "Stripper" or "Pussy Rap" would seem a natural response as stripper or sex worker is a persona adapted by female performers in art, music, and film. We'll see other femme rappers occasionally give a lap dance or wink at bisexuality. That Cardi is openly and unapologetically both, has opened the lane for other women and artists to be their most authentic selves.

It's also worth noting that while male rappers could be braggadocious or openly just lie about criminality to build their allure, Cardi's brushes with the NYPD and alleged behavior (the same that would eventually land her a role in the JLo-fronted film *Hustlers* about a ring of strippers with ambition and roofies) is still something she is criticized for.

Producer Jermaine Dupree likened the proliferation of new type of femme rappers to strippers in an interview with *People* magazine. In response Cardi went on *The Breakfast Club* where she and the host defended a spectrum of talented femmes and what they chose to rap about. She noted that women who weren't singing about pussy weren't really getting supported and that she had variety in her catalog.[8]

[8]Jermaine Dupri Calls Today's Female Rappers "Strippers Rapping," Cardi B Claps Back.

Until Cardi's ascension, stripping was not deemed an acceptable career path to fame. Many women who engaged in sex work prior to success in the arts were stigmatized, blackmailed, or shunned. Porn stars and strippers could obtain a certain level of notoriety, however, and during the 1990s well until the streaming era, porn offered the most generous wage compensation for women in a professional field, where they outearned their male counterparts ten to one. Some of these porn stars were able to monetize themselves as a brand, but were rarely afforded the opportunity of mainstream work outside of their "porn star" persona and the women that were, were almost all exclusively white, and fit a narrowly specific definition of heteronormativity, and patriarchal beauty standards. The level of acceptance between sex and pop culture would change quickly with the widespread commercial appeal of the celebrity sex tape.

These sometimes leaked, sometimes planted, captured intimacies became so common by the 2020s they warrant only a day or two of Twitter chatter. In the early aughts, they created a literal virtual explosion pushed forward by the newly expanding practice of internet downloads.

Music and the celeb sex tape would be intertwined first by Tommy Lee and Pamela Anderson whose private honeymoon suffered a real invasion of privacy.

In the DVD era, the notable recording that would forever cement home pornography as a cultural catalyst, the tape between musician Ray J and Kim Kardashian that would go on to launch her family's empire, set a new standard for celebrity sexualization, and broad cultural acceptance, making Kardashian the most monetarily successful groupie in music history.

Unsurprisingly, this pairing is a historically logical one, as sex-centric art and music were merged in the early twentieth century with the mainstreaming of burlesque and the advent of "the American Blues Woman" in pop culture. Both the movement-centric art form that originated in Victorian England and the platforming of femme Black musicians occur in unison around 1920 via Vaudeville, which offered segregated, touring, live entertainment across the country. Gertrude "Ma" Rainey is credited for creating the term "the blues" as part of her Black Vaudeville performances.

These frequent road performances which would, along with the expansion of technologies like phonographic records and piano-roll recordings, bring the first female Black "pop stars" like Mamie Smith, Bessie Smith, Alberta Hunter, and Victoria Spivy to a broad American audience. These recordings were one of the first mediums to vocalize the plights of Black women post slavery in America: their economic conditions, the complexity of their romantic lives, and struggles with addiction, all topics Black femme artists are still navigating 100 years later.

In its initial stages, burlesque was also a vehicle for social commentary often poking fun at social morays.[9] The art itself modified from centering on the comedic, to incorporating world and popular dance, to more overtly sexual moves over the course of its time in America.

[9]https://vaudeville.sites.arizona.edu/node/30

Burlesque performers began performing dances that involved greater levels of sexual display—the cooch dance, a modified belly dance that was introduced to the United States at the 1893 Chicago World's Columbian Exposition, was incorporated into burlesque performances, followed by the shimmy of the 1910s. This progression eventually culminated in the ultimate performance of sexual exhibition—the striptease of the 1920s and 1930s.[10]

By 2020, Cardi's throne would be sitting squarely at the interaction of comedy, stripping, and capitalism's impact on the femme, Black American experience. It was this combination that also made her the perfect fit for *Playboy* magazine and their new platform, *Centerfold*. In the winter of 2021 after the Hefners left *Playboy*, the magazine sought a new, femme forward image and offered Cardi their first ever role as Creative Director in Residence.[11] *Centerfold* was meant to be a competitor to *Only Fans*, a platform used by sex workers to interact with and directly monetize fan interaction.

By shattering the stigma of sex work in entertainment and offering femmes a chance to earn money on their own terms and invest in their art and themselves, Cardi afforded the next generation of performers to dictate their futures without shame, making sure the new girls won't have to get up ten times to make it.

[10]Ibid.
[11]https://remezcla.com/culture/cardi-b-playboy-first-creative-director-in-residence/

2

Drip

In 1699, *The First English Dictionary of Slang* was published. Its author EB Gentleman sought to educate upper-class Londoners on the "canting" verbiage of the lower classes. Its relevancy is explained in an editorial description of the text by the University of Chicago Press:

> This dictionary is also the first that attempts to show the overlap and integration between canting words and common slang words. Refusing to distinguish between criminal vocabulary and the more ordinary everyday English of the period, it sets canting words side by side with terms used in domestic culture and those used by sailors and laborers. With such a democratic attitude toward words, this text is genuinely a modern dictionary, as well as the first attempt by dictionary makers to catalog the ever-changing world of English slang.[1]

[1]https://press.uchicago.edu/ucp/books/book/distributed/F/bo10609627.html

By 1999, some 300 years later, Hip-Hop would firmly occupy the spot as the strongest force intermingling cultural and class and influencing modern language.

We've long used familiarity with new slang to distinguish general hipness and as a litmus test of cultural awareness. There are very few in American society regardless of age, class, or race that aren't familiar with Snoop Dog's "fo' shizzle," or adding "izzle" as a distinguishable suffix. You will catch the oldest and whitest among us still "izzling" to sometimes cringe-worthy results.

In 2018, the year *Invasion of Privacy* was released, the website Genius would explore the nearly 2000 percent lyrical increase in the slang term "drip" from its 2010 origins.[2] The site credits the term in its current usage as defined by *Dictionary.com*'s Slang section as "when you've got *the drip* or are *dripping*, it means in slang that your look or style is extremely fashionable or sexy"[3] to Houston rapper Sauce Walka.[4] Walka's usage is a variation on the longer used term "sauce" for those who roll with high-end, designer, swagger.

The relationship between high-end luxury brands and Hip-Hop is logical as explained by filmmaker Sacha Jenkins who documented Hip-Hop fashions evolution in the 2015 documentary *Fresh Dressed*. Jenkins told *LA Times* writer Max Berlinger:

[2]https://genius.com/a/what-does-drip-mean
[3]https://www.dictionary.com/e/slang/drip/#:~:text=If%20you%20have%20
the%20drip,You're%20on%20point.
[4]https://genius.com/a/what-does-drip-mean
The *Genius* pieces date the first usages of "drip or dripping" to Lil Keke in 1996 and Wu-Tang Clan's Ghostface Killer in 2000.

Fashion has always been an important part of the Hip Hop identity because fashion has always been an important part of black identity in America, because when you don't have much ownership over where you can land in society, your financial situation, your educational situation, the one thing you can control is the way you look.[5]

In the piece, stylist Matthew Hensen added:

Our culture has aspects that are rooted in looking good despite having little to nothing to work with and making the best of it, and this comes from the church experience. You wear your best. That transcends to now—being proud of your appearance. Not only be good at what you do, but you have to look the part to be seen as an equal.[6]

The beginnings of luxury brands and Hip-Hop are credited to Harlem's Dapper Dan who would "knock off" high-end designers in his 1980s creations that would be "ubiquitous with Hip Hop." For the *New York Times*, author Nelson George described Dapper Dan's work:

His custom-made clothing defined so-called ghetto glamour as it married designer logos with patterns, colors and cuts reflecting the taste of young, street-savvy African-Americans. If Andy Warhol became famous for appropriating a Campbell's soup can, "Dap" was celebrated

[5]https://www.latimes.com/entertainment/la-et-ms-ig-Hip Hop-fashion-streets-couture-20180125-htmlstory.html
[6]Ibid.

for taking labels like Gucci and Fendi and remixing them in a style that was bolder than anything coming out of Paris or Milan. And his style became ubiquitous; classic Hip Hop albums (by the likes of Eric B. & Rakim and LL Cool J) featured Dapper Dan outfits on their covers. Just as Hip Hop in '88 was starting to emerge as a major influence on mainstream American culture, the Dapper Dan take on fashion was already being imitated, emulated and ripped off.[7]

Dapper Dan not only dressed the men of early Hip-Hop. Salt, Peppa, and Spinderella's iconic gold, red, and green leather ensembles are pure "Dap" and a prime example of how early women rappers used gender neutrality in fashion as a means of equity. The custom suits showcase boxy shoulders over form-fitting leotards to create a slightly more feminized version of what their male counterparts were wearing.

Just as women's lyrical impact began to influence Hip-Hop culture, shifts to their personal style would begin to break through. In a piece for *Bonafide Magazine* writer Leke Sanusi writes:

> If rap gave voice to the rumblings of America's disadvantaged young, black and gifted, then fashion helped tailor their message; presenting an irresistible, eye-catching show of youthful rebellion and exuberance to the world. For the likes of MC Lyte and Roxanne Shanté, sporting cut-off shorts and gold door-knocker earrings

[7]https://www.nytimes.com/2019/07/09/books/review/dapper-dan-daniel-r-day.html?smid=url-share

amounted to much more than just a fashion statement—it
was a political one, too; the defiantly swagged out rappers
of the '80s wearing their hearts, homes and blackness on
their sleeves as expressions of their identity and pride.[8]

Writer Hattie Collins in a piece titled "2017 Was the Year
Female Rappers Got Their Due" noted that "Sha-Rock's
successors had to physically 'toughen up' and wear masculine
fashions in order to be taken as seriously as their male peers."
So it would make sense that as women took control of
their sexuality in their lyrics, the feminization of their fashion
would also follow suit.

*****

For me, inspiration comes from everywhere and starts as
a daydream. When I was a pre-teen, the radio only played
Hip Hop on Fridays and Saturdays and was hosted by Mr.
Magic & Kool DJ Red Alert. I would sit on the floor by
the radio with my cassette tapes and record the music
and while listening I envisioned wardrobe. There weren't
many visuals out at that time; basically, there were none.
So you had to sit and imagine what these rappers looked
like, what they should wear, what I would wear, and what
my friends would wear.

—Misa Hylton[9]

[8]https://www.bonafidemag.com/dressed-ill-hip-hop-conquered-fashion-world/
[9]https://www.billboard.com/music/music-news/misa-hylton-Hip Hop-style-interview-8039207/

Misa Hylton grew up in Mount Vernon, NY, the intersection of NYC and Westchester county, around six miles north of the Bronx. Her early obsession with Hip-Hop led to what would be a lifelong career at seventeen, when while assisting on an Uptown Records video, she convinced Andre Harell to let the featured act adopt a more "street" aesthetic with backwards baseball caps, combat boots, and hoodies.[10] It's hard to imagine Jodeci becoming known as "the bad boys of R&B" if they had chosen to "suit up" like many of their contemporaries.

Hylton's innovation led to her working with other *Uptown* artists and very soon after she would meet her muse and style soul sister Lil' Kim. Their first meeting is the stuff true girl love is made of—and the birthplace of a shift in pop culture-admiration of each other's style.

The two soon struck up a friendship that would lead to one of the most iconic ensembles in MTV history (Hylton is the designer of Kim's iconic lavender 1999 VMAs jumpsuit and styled her overall) and bringing hyper-femininity to Hip-Hop.

In a live conversation with *Complex* magazine titled "The Naked Truth, How Lil Kim Changed Hip Hop Fashion," Kim and Hylton reminisced about their first meeting recounting Kim's look, her short hair, and wearing a cute vest that made her say "who is that?" with Kim adding of Hylton "she was so beautiful, I wanna be like her." From the moment they saw each other their first thoughts were of each other's "flyness"

---

[10] *Vibe.com* x Women in Hip-Hop w/ Misa Hylton (Fashion Icon).

and one of the most powerful forces that would shape high and commercial fashion was born.

In most tellings of Misa Hylton's story, the first name that will be mentioned is her high school boyfriend and co-parent of son Justin Dior, Sean Combs. But if you research Hylton, you'll find her love and knowledge of Hip-Hop have benefited the art form as much as the man who would become Diddy. In a video interview with *Vibe* magazine's Jazzie Belle, she shares her love of Hip-Hop dates back to her childhood in the 1970s and she could still, today, recite all the lyrics of Sugar Hills Gang's classic "Rapper's Delight."

The cover promotional art for Kim's debut *Hardcore* features her squatting in a Pat Field's leopard fur bikini purchased by Hylton in the designer's Manhattan boutique, which both she and Kim frequented.[11] Fields would later go on to be one of the most seminal forces in 2000s fashion as the lead stylist on *Sex & the City*, which would also, despite its flaws, prove to be a force in feminist sexual liberation.

The assumption was that Kim's image was being crafted by the men in her musical periphery to sell sex, when in fact, she and Hylton pushed for ownership of their unique femme identity as their own.

Culture critic and famed writer bell hooks critiqued Kim's image in a 1997 interview with *Paper* magazine where the feminist luminary and the young rapper discussed her debut:

> In pictures, Lil' Kim looks like the images that used to appear in the sleazy black porn magazine *Players*. As

[11]The Naked Truth: How Lil Kim Changed Hip-Hop Fashion | *ComplexCon*(versations).

teenagers, we used to laugh at those pictures. Women in them were always "overdone." Sometimes they looked like raggedy drag queens—a bit rough around the edges. As representations of the hyper-femme, they called out the lack of imagination in sexist, straight male fantasies. Naturally, it's been a bit puzzling to me to see "old" stuff revamped as new and daring. The only new thing happening here is that it took so long for a Hip Hop girl to make the down-and-dirty talk pay her bills big-time. Mark my words. Long before Lil' Kim could speak, smart sluts of all ages were talking trash. To talk trash and get paid has always been harder for women than for men. This 21-year-old has gone where others have not been able to go, 'cause she's got the right dudes behind her.[12]

While it's true Kim's entry into Rap is essentially through male gatekeeping, in the 1990s there was no other path. Taking the risk to be the truest, most daringly authentic version of herself is the first foot step in what will be Cardi's diamond-studded runway.

*****

June Ambrose, like Cardi, is an island girl, from the Bronx. Her path to music styling couldn't have been more different than Misa Hylton's.

An Antigua native, she went from flirting with investment banking to an internship with *MCA* Records where she fell

[12]https://www.papermag.com/lil-kim-bell-hooks-cover-1427357106.html?r ebelltitem=3#rebelltitem3

in love with styling artists. An essential part of the magical Hype Williams formula providing the fashion in front of the fish eye lens. Her clients would include Missy, Mariah, Mary J, and Alicia. When Jay-Z needed to look as good as Beyoncé for the *On the Run* tours, Ambrose, his longtime stylist, was on the case. Her approach was different from the stylists who came before her as she told the *Hollywood Reporter* that "[she] didn't come up under another stylist or costume designer, I came up from the theater. Most of the artists felt like they had to be themselves because they were telling poetic narratives from their lives." By contrast, she thought, "'Let's imagine the person that you want to become'—that was life-changing because it helped them to separate their personal personas from their artistic personas, and it gave them just a little bit more space to play." As Blige tells *THR*, "Beyond being one of the best stylists of our time, she gives you the freedom to feel great about doing you."

Selling Hip-Hop femininity would boom in the early aughts due in good part to the work of Kimora Lee Simmons, who at thirteen was the first mixed race model to walk for Chanel.

It all started with a simple, well-fitting T-shirt with a sizable feline logo. *Baby Phat* began as an offshoot of Russell Simmons's Phat Farm Collection and became a massive fashion force. It marks one of the first times women of color making clothes for women of color crosses over into a brand mass audience fell in love with.

Femme athletic wear collections and Hip-Hop would soon become synonymous.

*****

Though Cardi's roots made for a sensible early first collaboration with Fashion Nova, she quickly became the "it girl" and muse for several designers. If slaying designer fashion were actual murder, Cardi's ride-or-die in crime would be Kollin Carter, her longtime stylist. His keen eye has steered her toward her most memorable moments.

Christian Siriano would be one of the first to dress Cardi, crafting some of her most memorable looks, including her gothy all-black, "hair skirt," pregnancy reveal dress on *SNL*, and a white cone bra jumpsuit that is Cardi to a T—the perfect blend of Material Girl-meets-Fly Girl.

For her 2019 Grammy takeover, Cardi and Kollin would pull from vintage Mugler.[13] Her performance attire, which included a black body stocking with a large tail feather piece and headwear, her artful pink and black "Venus" gown she walked the carpet on, and the white-fringed gown she would be the first woman to win *Rap Album of Year* in were all pulled from Mugler's 1997 collection. She would pair with the designer in the fall of 2021 to win Paris Fashion Week sporting vintage and contemporary looks from the designer's collection all week. She would even go on to name drop the designer in her collaboration with Normandi, "Wildside."

And, of course, no one since the dressed by Pat Field's icon Carrie Bradshaw has done more to sell $800 shoes than Cardi B. The signature scarlet soles of Christian Louboutin will forever be synonymous with "Bodak Yellow." The summer

[13]https://fashionista.com/2021/10/cardi-b-vintage-thierry-mugler-grammys-2019

of 2017 would see as reported by *Ranker* that "According to a recent report from *Business of Fashion* and *Lyst*, searches for the luxury label's heels have increased by a staggering 217 percent since 'Bodak Yellow' first hit the airwaves."[14]

Louboutin didn't know who Cardi was in 2017, but by 2021 they were pals.

In 2020, he virtually awarded her the *Footwear News'* "Style Influencer of the Year Award" noting:

> Her freedom, her liberty of speech and basically her commitment to everything [makes Cardi B stand out] … She stands and fights for what she believes in, she's the opposite of politically correct. Either you adore that or you hate it, but you cannot stay indifferent. What probably makes her so influential at the moment is she's authentic and people actually respond to that, and that's a very good thing.[15]

[14]https://www.racked.com/2017/11/20/16658444/cardi-b-christian-louboutin
[15]https://www.yahoo.com/video/happened-cardi-b-met-christian-220209222.html?guccounter=1&guce_referrer=aHR0cHM6Ly93d3cuZ29vZ2xlLmNvbVS8&guce_referrer_sig=AQAAAB1LcXDtJOyGnjJnyqeDbqK9HEbpU_uJv_pmV0T1dW8DjSMbfni2h8ixWTiT92JqTUG81-TVqlJPDrn3QmFyPbSUAAVDhnm7zE4FTQoIt9bEcWHHT1KKdj9da8_zI4qi2YkkTNwbr-67UPxWaZ5o6ycpt606Z6ICfViQjfnnaACy

3

Bickenhead

There is no square inch of the human body with more nerve endings than the clitoris.

Nestled in the vulva, this tiny organ is unique in that it seemingly has no biological purpose other than pleasure.

It can be stimulated with water, orally, manually, and with vibration, including those from deep bass tones as evidenced by numerous YouTube videos of young women giving throbbing beats a new meaning as they achieve orgasm via intense subwoofers in tricked-out rides. These bass-driven stimulations cause a state of arousal drawing blood away from the brain to foment in the clitoris. As Sir Mix-a-Lot rightfully pontificated on "My Posse's on Broadway," an 808-kick drum, given the right method of delivery, can in fact "make a girly get dumb."

Though the clit might be female physiology's most fun organ, it is just one in the external vulva anatomy. The quick Wikipedia recap states:

The vulva (plural: vulvas or vulvae; derived from Latin for wrapper or covering) consists of the external female sex organs. The vulva includes the mons pubis (or mons veneris), labia majora, labia minora, clitoris, vestibular bulbs, vulval vestibule, urinary meatus, the vaginal opening, hymen, and Bartholin's and Skene's vestibular glands. The urinary meatus is also included as it opens into the vulval vestibule. Other features of the vulva include the pudendal cleft, sebaceous glands, the urogenital triangle (anterior part of the perineum), and pubic hair. The vulva includes the entrance to the vagina, which leads to the uterus, and provides a double layer of protection for this by the folds of the outer and inner labia. Pelvic floor muscles support the structures of the vulva.[1]

Though vital, the vulva is rarely addressed by her given name in popular culture. The vulvic area is often mistakenly referred to as "the vagina," seeming to discount the fact that the vaginal cavity is an internal organ. British slang popularized the word "cunt," though its origins can be traced back to ancient times. Feminist theorist Inga Muscio in her 2002 work, *Cunt: A Declaration of Independence* writes:

In ancient writings the word for "cunt" was synonymous with "woman," though not in the insulting modern sense. An Egyptologist was shocked to find the maxims of Ptah-Hotep "used for 'woman' a term that was more than blunt," though its indelicacy was not in the eye of the ancient beholder, only in that of the modern scholar … The word "cunt" originates from many early words in the languages of various nations. These nations are India,

[1]Vulva—*Wikipedia.*

Ireland, China, Rome, and Egypt. These words were "titles of respect for women, priestesses and witches." Also these words were derivatives of various goddesses' names.[2]

The early 2010s saw a feminist exploration of the word with publications like *Bitch* magazine and popular online forum *Jezebel* in pieces titled "A Fascinating History of the 'C-Word'"[3] and "'Cunt' Should Not Be a Bad Word."[4]

But just a few years later, feminist cultural focus would shift to more popular American terminology, and a word estimated by *lyrics.com* to be found in over 3,400 songs in popular music, a word as abhorrent to some as it is adored by others, pussy.[5]

With its origins not as well recorded as cunt, pussy is believed by some to be derived from the Old Norse "Puss" meaning pocket pouch and brought to popularity through modern pornography.[6] Merriam-Webster's Kory Stamper told *The Huffington Post*, "The etymology of 'pussy' isn't known definitively, which seems odd but is somewhat

[2]Muscio, Inga. *Cunt: A Declaration of Independence.* Berkeley: Seal Press, 2002. Print.
[3]Zoladz, Lindsay. "A Fascination History of the 'C-Word'." *Bitch* magazine. n.p., n.d. Web. Dec. 10, 2014.
[4]Baker, Katie. "'Cunt' Should Not Be a Bad Word." *Jezebel.* Feb. 27, 2013. Web. Dec. 10, 2014.
[5]Pussy of course has a duel, more derogatory meaning, cowardes, and some of the aforementioned songs containing the word are using it in this context. Author's note.
[6]Engele, Gigi. "Where Does the Word Pussy Come from and Should Feminists Really Use It?" *Glamour.* Apr. 24, 2017.

common with taboo words."[7] Webster also notes pussy became a vulgarity around 1699, with *pussy* meaning: (1) vulva, (2a) sexual intercourse, and (2b) the female partner in sexual intercourse.[8]

Pussy shows up in popular recorded music around 1931 in a deluge of jazzy, feline-centric, double entendres, by a British clarinetist and bandleader Harry Roy and His Bat Club Boys and their hit "My Girl's Pussy."

Some ninety odd years later, many, many, men would go on to sing about pussy.

Getting it.

Leaving it.

Owning it.

Selling it.

Absolutely not, then, enthusiastically, eating it.

Telling us it's so good it renders them powerless and not responsible for their actions.

Telling us it's not shit.

And it's not just Hip-Hop. You'll find folk, country, death metal, punk, and good old rock & roll songs full of men and their opinions on pussy.

Listen to them all: you'll find Prince is, seemingly, the only one who actually does pussy any justice at all.

Enter Kimberly Denise Jones.

---

[7]Brooks, Katherine. "Where the Hell Does the Word Pussy Come From?" *The Huffington Post.* Oct. 12, 2016. 08:28am EDT.
[8]Japrose Hill, Andrew. "Flap over Wap: A Brief History of 'Pussy' from Fairy Tale to Hip Hop to Culture-Wars Flashpoint." *Medium.* Sept. 7, 2020.

Starting as a teen in The Notorious B.I.G.'s Junior MAFIA, Jones, or as she is more famously known, Lil' Kim wasn't the first woman to express her sexuality through music but her reclamation of pussy from her male contemporaries marks a distinct cultural shift. Her 1996 debut *Hardcore* would become the first inspiration for the genre that by the 2010s would be known as "Pussy Rap," but in the anti-feminist backlash of the late 1990s, it served as a beacon for moral outrage.

In conversation with intersectional feminist icon bell hooks for *Paper* magazine in 1997, Kim addressed the controversy:

bh: A lot of people are talking about you as an example of sexy feminism, as a liberated woman. What do you think? Do you think you represent the liberated woman or the sexy girl of men's fantasies?

LK: Both. The reason I say both is that we have been set back–everybody says that. Sometimes they say I set back women's liberation.

bh: I don't think that, but go ahead.

LK: I don't think that either. You wanna know why? Because we have people like Too Short, Luke Skyywalker (of 2 Live Crew) Biggie (Smalls). Elvis Presley, Prince, who are very, very, very sexual, and they don't get trashed because they do it. But all the sudden we have a female, who happens to be a rapper, like, me, and my doing it is wrong. And "cause I like doing it's even more wrong because we fight for years as women to do the same things men are doing."[9]

[9] hooks, bell. "Hardcore Honey: bell hooks Goes on the Down Low with Lil' Kim." *Paper* magazine. 1997.

The year 2016, exactly twenty years after the release of *Hardcore*, would mark the most significant shift in the epidemiology of pussy and pop culture when a candidate for president of the United States made "grab 'em by the pussy" a household phrase, thus setting off a wave of mainstream pussy talk the likes of which Lil' Kim had never ventured. Issa Rae's brilliant HBO comedy *Insecure*'s 2016 debut episode sees her character, an aspiring rapper, freestyling about her bestie's "broken pussy," a joke that would run till the conclusion of the series' 5 seasons.

Though Kim is the originator, it's Florida rapper Trina who would give us the designer drenched formula on her hit 2000 record *Da Baddest Bitch* and the under-acknowledged "Pull Over" and themes that would make up Pussy Rap's notable characteristics.

Have you mentioned your thighs and ass? Are they thick? CHECK. Proceed.

Are you a bad bitch? CHECK. Proceed.

Would you rate your face a "Ten?" CHECK. Proceed.

Is your waist slim? CHECK. Proceed.

Is your ass fat? CHECK. Proceed.

Is your sexual prowess aka pussy game so on point you can assess it a high monetary value? Is it worth a truck? A mansion? CHECK. Proceed.

Can you twerk to it? CHECK. Proceed.

Are you a freak? CHECK. Proceed.

Are you the very baddest bitch? CHECK. Proceed.

Does your badness shame other hoes? CHECK. Proceed. Again.

Is your ass the absolute fattest?

Does it get you cash?

CHECK. Proceed.

CONGRATULATIONS! You've just made Pussy Rap.

Femme Rap had, of course, been fluid in Pussy-ology before white suburban moms were knitting pussy hats in performative political protest.

Nicki Minaj used her singular dominance of the genre for nearly a decade to push and play with the boundaries of pussy and pop. Flamboyant and fabulous stylist to the stars Law Roach blends Hip-Hop iconography and high-end couture, all while imploring all of us to be something beyond opulent, beyond decadent, beyond the beyond, he demands nothing less than that we "Make.It.Pussy."

Cardi B, hard at work on what would become *Invasion of Privacy* was listening.

"Bickenhead," much like pussy culture, is about reclamation. A reworking of the Project Pat classic "Chickenhead," it is a humorous and hooky diss track meant to draw off 1990s stereotypes about low-income Black women. The song keeps it lighthearted, however. The levity comes in the form of a femme response delivered by pioneering female rapper, Three 6 Mafia's LaChat, to all of Pat's criticism of the women he deems chickenheads, dismissing him with the "Boy. Please. Whatever." line retained in the "Bickenhead" chorus.

He criticizes her budget hair extensions, and her judgment for buying an outfit instead of paying her light bill. She criticizes the money he spends on custom rims for his Cadillac and his judgment when his gas tank is on EMPTY and takes a shot at his worn out, cheap shoes. LaChat's retort adds equity to the track and keeps it from veering into easy misogyny.

The production is minimal and low-fi, the hi-hat clocking in at an easy 4/4 tempo. The synth line, mimicking strings drives the melody and highlights Pat's southern, punctuated delivery style. Cardi takes the bones of this classic and slaps the proverbial and literal pussy all over them.

"Bickenhead" declares itself a completely different animal from the get go.

Where "Chickenhead" explores the confines of poverty, "Bickenhead" revels in the lux.

The production by Grammy-winning duo Ayo and Keyz and Kentucky Producer Nes is polished to precision. The hi-hat is crisp and owns the front of the mix. The original hook is dropped to a deeper octave and the bass is given a disjointed distortion making for an eerie, more sinister vibe. Project Pat's signature "alllllllright" from the track echoes like a ghost in the background.

Before we can question where the track is headed, Cardi chimes in to let us know this track is specifically for her international, nasty hoes with luxury apartments, high-priced lawyers, and nemesis who best watch their backs. She implores other women with less means[10] through the course of the song to empower themselves financially by any means necessary and stop hating on her good fortune. Is she to blame for being "naturally gorgeous, genetically gifted and in

---

[10]The Urban Dictionary offers one definition of a "Birkenhead" as someone who complains about being poor.

contact with her father?" she posits, concluding you would have to be unattractive and unemployed to hate her or key her Lamborghini truck.

But it's verse three where Cardi's pussy game is significantly upped, by offering tips as how, when, and where femmes looking to up their financial situation should "pop their pussy."

To clarify, the *Urban Dictionary*[11] offers several definitions of "pussy popping." The most common is a dance move that sees a woman bent over, hands on the ground and ass in the air shaking it front to back found most prominently in Twerking. The dance, with origins in West Africa and the Caribbean, had took off in New Orleans and eventually took on stylized variations in American cities. In Atlanta, twerking migrated to the Strip clubs as it did in Miami, creating the hybrid contemporary version that constitutes the most poppin' pussy variety.

Earlier definitions are both patriarchal and contradictory, sermonizing pussy popping is either a characteristic of the Madonna (an intact hymen) or the whore (a labia so loose it claps). The femme reclamation of pussy sees the terms defined by the late 2010s become celebratory—"the art of thrusting your pelvis in and out to prove an item worthy of your awesomeness" and when something is the "most lit" or really great it is "Pussy Poppin" and offering up "Pussy Popping Power" as the femme equivalent of "Big

---

[11]Urban Dictionary: Pussy poppin.

Dick Energy."[12] "Pussy popping" could also be "a kegel,"[13] an exercise meant to strengthen the pelvic floor and kegel muscle responsible for bladder control and gripping and clenching the penis during hetero sex. You'll hear kegels referenced in the rhyme scheme of many femme rappers.

"The Bickenhead" "how's'" of popping one's pussy include like it's been a long time, like it's almost no longer fashionable, and making it "slip the slide" (like you're from Miami aka "the 305" home of seminal southern label Slip-N-Slide Records), and making it smile.

The suggested "where's": the pole, the stove (?) and "when"—at work, at church, and, why not, while you drive.

Pussy will be mentioned on *Invasion of Privacy* just under thirty times by that exact name and more by others. Some like Vag & Bag are too good to not take advantage of the rhyme scheme.

There are certainly other records that have used the term more hardily.

Cardi's skill is using pussy handedly.

Declaring her own to be so good it makes her say "Cardi" when she comes on "I Do," the album's final track, it is one of the most often-quoted and memorable pussy references; but it's "Bickenhead's" repetition of the term in verse three,

---

[12] Big Dick Energy is a term coined on twitter to memorialize the later chef Anthony Bourdain. "How Big Dick Energy Explains Modern Masculinity." *Vox*, https://www.vox.com/culture/2018/6/27/17506898/big-dick-energy-explained. Accessed Oct. 19, 2023.

[13] "Kegel exercises." *Merriam-Webster.com Dictionary*, Merriam-Webster, https://www.merriam-webster.com/dictionary/Kegel%20exercises. Accessed Mar. 31, 2022.

dropping it eleven times in around 22 seconds, in a way so hooky and fun it seemingly neutralized the term's negative connotations, giving permission for even the most timid listener to embrace "the pop" like she was merely asking them to shake their asses or put a hand in the air.

Of course it's not just about pussy. Its detractors will point to what makes Pussy Rap unpalatable is the gushing overtness of its sexual content as if men had not said whatever they wanted to in terms of sexuality, violence, and morality judgments about women since they began to sing. We've listened for years as men told us all about their hard, big dicks, in song. Suddenly when femme rappers brag about vaginal lubrication, i.e., "wetness" as a measurable and boastable standard of their own pleasure it's deemed "too much" by men in the game.

Women praising their own vaginal fortitude is a hard reminder that it's the femmiest femmes for whom pleasure is exclusively theirs. Lyrically, Pussy Rap reminds you femmes are actually the ones who get it, who leave it, who own it, who sell it, who can be down with enthusiastically eating it, and who know it's so good it renders you stupid.

So tell us again how it's not shit?

In April of 2020, two years after *Invasion of Privacy* was released, the Supreme Court granted Seattle rock band Thunderpussy copyrighted ownership of their name, in a landmark case for monikers deemed "scandalous" under Section 2(a) of the 1946 Lanham Act[14] that set the measure of vulgarity in a copyright request.

---

[14]"Thunderpussy" Band Granted Trademark | *Law & Crime* (lawandcrime.com).

And though we'll never know if Justice Elena Kagan has ever popped her pussy like it was going out of style, she did offer the majority opinion, stating:

"The First Amendment does not allow the government to penalize views just because many people, whether rightly or wrongly, see them as offensive," Kagan said from the bench in announcing the decision. "The most fundamental principle of free speech law is that the government can't penalize or disfavor or discriminate against expression based on the ideas or viewpoints it conveys."[15]

By August of the same year, Cardi would solidify the mainstreaming of pussy by bringing it to the number one position on *Billboard* Top 100 in her collaboration with Houston rap phenomenon Megan Thee Stallion on "WAP," aka "Wet Ass Pussy." The track extended her record as the female rapper with the most number-one singles and was declared by *Billboard* "one of the most dominant Hot 100 number ones of the last 30 years."[16]

Make it pussy, indeed.

[15]Ibid.

[16]Anderson, Trevor. "Cardi B & Megan Thee Stallion's 'WAP' Is One of the Most Dominant Hot 100 No. 1s of Last 30 Years." *Billboard.* Aug. 18, 2020. Archived from the original on Aug. 29, 2020. Retrieved Sept. 8, 2020.

4

Bodak Yellow

1. Cardi B, "Bodak Yellow" It's amazing that Cardi's beautiful bundle of trash talk made it all the way to No. 1 without a traditional hook—until you realize that every phrase she blurts has its own ticklish melody, its own whiplash rhythm. She doesn't need a hook. She's pure musicality.[1]
—*The Washington Post*, naming *Bodak Yellow* the Song of 2017.

Ruled by Venus, those born under the Sun sign Libra are often the "it girls" of the Zodiac.[2]

Given to indulgence, Libra often covet opulence and seek luxury and high-end items.[3]

---

[1]https://www.washingtonpost.com/lifestyle/style/best-music-of-2017-cardi-b-paints-the-world-bodak-yellow/2017/12/06/cad4d6be-d5fc-11e7-95bf-df7c19270879_story.html
[2]Fabulous at Every Age: Famous Libra Celebrities You Should Know (*harpersbazaar.com.sg*), Oct. 9, 2017.
[3]Libra Women Traits | *LoveToKnow*.

Ruled by the Scales of Justice, Libras seek balance, but when presented with difficult options can become indecisive.[4]

Libras, when they believe they are wronged, they are quick to dismiss those who cross them rather than deal with confrontation.[5]

If the above feels familiar, pull up "Bodak Yellow" and read along as the first verse plays.

Born on October 11, Cardi B is a Libra, so it should come as no surprise her international anthem, one of the biggest in the history of popular music, viewed well over 1 billion times on YouTube, drips with all the marked characteristics of the Zodiac's seventh sign.

When asked by *Vogue* magazine "What's the most accurate trait of you as a Libra?" her answer was quick.

"We are very ambitious. We love working. We love making new money. Also it's really hard for us to make choices."

As it's also in Libra's nature to deconstruct something and rebuild it in their own image, it would make sense "Bodak Yellow" takes the bed of Kodak Black's "No Flockin'" and builds something more opulent, feminine, and modern while still careful to mine the best aspects of the original.

It's unapologetically, scorching hot pink.

Lifting a beat or hook and making it your own is often done with a spirit of generosity, sometimes paying the original artist more than the original work earned, reviving them with a new audience and boosting back catalog activity. The same can be said of mimicked inflection. Sometimes it's a tribute, a way to show how another artist's work has inspired you.

[4]Libra Zodiac Sign: Characteristics, Dates, & More | *Astrology.com*.
[5]Terms of Libra-*Twitter*.

Sometimes, of course, it's a diss, a quick and easy hit job to say "not only can I do what you do, I can do it better than you" or because your beef is so big you'll pay your enemy (by using beats or music they created) to mock them.

It's prevalent enough that it has its own term. Interpolation. Interpolation distinguishes itself from sampling as it's a recreation of the original work. It can be accomplished musically by reworking an established song into another, or vocally by replicating an established flow. In most genres, but in Hip-Hop especially, cadence can be copyrighted.

Almost as messy as sampling disputes can be, interpolation has kept entertainment lawyers eating well for decades. Recently we can look to Olivia Rodrigo's "good 4 you" as an example of costly legal consequences of borrowing a hook.

While a guitar riff can be easily tweaked to cover a musician's ass legally, vocal delivery and cadence are much harder to covertly appropriate. *E! Online* broke down how much it cost Rodrigo to pay vocal homage to Paramore's Hayley Williams.

When Olivia Rodrigo gave Paramore and Taylor Swift songwriting credits on her *SOUR* hits, she wasn't just sharing the glory. She was sharing the sweet profits.

In fact, Rodrigo and her producer and co-writer, Dan Nigro, have given up more than $2 million in songwriting royalties on "good 4u," "deja vu," and "1 step forward, 3 steps back" after crediting the big names that inspired her, according to *Billboard*.

News broke a week ago that Rodrigo, 18, had retroactively credited Paramore singer Hayley Williams and former guitarist Joshua Farro for interpolating

"Misery Business" when she wrote "good 4 u," which was released in May.

Billboard estimates the banger has made at least $2.4 million in global publishing royalties so far, leaving Williams and Farro to split their share of $1.2 million. Nigro and Rodrigo split the other $1.2 million.[6]

As you would expect from the sign represented by the scales "Bodak Yellow" as a track is about balance. Cardi takes Kodak Black's delivery and strikes the perfect balance of veracity and bellicosity. Her pace could be likened to prize fighting. With punctuation and polish, she rolls line to line, verbal blows one after the other, holding the spotlight center stage for the entire track and she never so much as smudges her lip gloss in the process.

That Libra equity can also be found in the musicality of the song.

The track's engineer Evan Le Ray told *Sound on Sound* about balancing a mix with no "middle":

'Bodak Yellow' was mixed over three days at Fight Club, with producer J. White present for some of the time. "J. White did the beat and Cardi wrote the song, and the other people mentioned in the credits were helping out, but essentially it's Cardi's song. She also gave a credit to Kodak Black, because the song is based on one of his songs and she used his flow. With this track, J. White and everyone

[6]https://www.eonline.com/news/1301100/breaking-down-the-brutal-price-of-olivia-rodrigo-and-paramores-songwriting-controversy#:~:text=Olivia%20Rodrigo%20reportedly%20lost%20out,to%20Paramore%20and%20Taylor%20Swift

else wanted me to do less. Mainly they wanted to make sure that the energy was still there. As I said, the track is about the vocals, the 808 and the hi-hats. There's no mid-range, and nothing in the track to compete with the vocals. The only two problems I was dealing with were the synth, which was peeking out too much, so I had to put on some limiting and compression and spread it to the sides, plus I had to find a happy medium between the vocals being too low—meaning that when the kick hits, it drowns her out—or too high, in which case you don't feel the 808s.

"When I first got the session in, it was just a two-track and the vocals. So I spent a day going through the six vocal takes, leveling everything, and cleaning up pops and clicks and background noises. The producer flew in a couple of days later and we spent the entire day selecting the best vocal takes and comping them, and then finding the right balance between the vocals, the 808 and the hi-hats. That was the most important thing. I also needed to make sure that the rhythm track was locking, that the kicks were hitting, and so on. For the rest it was a matter of some EQ here and there, and leveling and panning. Throughout that day J. White worked on his laptop, using Logic, so some of the effects on the vocals, like delays and reverbs, come from that."[7]

Where as Kodak Black's version sounds as swampy and as Floridian as its creator, J. White Did It's production and Le Ray's precision give "Bodak Yellow" a pointedly Middle

[7]https://www.soundonsound.com/techniques/inside-track-cardi-b-bodak-yellow

Eastern flavor, the synth line mimicking percussion with the intonation of an Arabian oud, a traditional stringed instrument. The song's movement also mimics the curves found in Andalusian classical music that merges Spanish and Arabic musical stylings.

Given the influence, filming the video in Abu Dhabi made sense. The shoot with director Picture Perfect leaned into the vibe as well. Cardi is on a camel. She pets exotic cats; the energy screams "Oil Money." Cardi made a personal financial investment in the video of around $20,000.

It was a brilliant money movie. The video would see her become the first female rapper to have two videos with 1 billion-plus views on YouTube and become one of the most viewed music videos in the platform's history.

Lyrics for the song, as it's told, were written mid-flight as Cardi visualized verbally bitch slapping her haters. Libras are a bit habitual and collaborative by nature, so she again worked with Pardison Fontaine to flush out the song lyrically.

Cardi's open use of a co-writer has only been weaponized by her critics since her early work, though she has been constantly transparent about her process. Ghostwriting or uncredited collaborations have famously been frowned on in Hip-Hop, the implication being your work is less than authentic if someone else's hands are in your rhymes.

In an early interview with Beats for Apple Music, Cardi clarified how Fontaine contributed to the process saying she strived to get better "at flowing":

> I needed a little bit of help breaking out of my box, I felt like my music, if you listen to my mixtape it is very trappy,

BODAK YELLOW

it was almost drill … I felt like I would never get out of that style, I'm so stuck on rapping like that. I needed to break that shell and indeed to flow a little bit easier and cleaner. I don't feel like I've perfected it yet, but I'm getting better and better and better.

It's the interpolation and her developed flow that *Rolling Stone* first notes when they named the song #32 on their list of the best songs of the 2010s:

The flow was borrowed from Kodak Black's "No Flockin,'" but the transformation of stress-mode fury into feminine glamour was pure Cardi. She wrote her rhymes on a plane, listening to a beat her producer J. White had sent her. "Every bitch that I don't like came to my head," she said. "And I pictured me, slapping it to them." Boasting about paying her mama's bills and dubbing red-bottom Louboutins "bloody shoes," she was a trapper with a double-dutch heart. When she knocked Taylor Swift's "Look What You Made Me Do" from the number-one spot—becoming the first solo female rapper to top the charts since Lauryn Hill two decades earlier—Swift sent her flowers to celebrate.—J.L.[8]

Billboard also heralded "Bodak Yellow" in its songs of the 2010s coverage:

[8]https://www.rollingstone.com/music/music-lists/the-100-best-songs-of-the-2010s-917532/cardi-b-bodak-yellow-single-917576/

Cardi B is heading into the 2020s still on top, scoring a Grammy for best rap album, a No. 1 album on the Billboard 200 with *Invasion of Privacy* in 2018, and two more Hot 100 No. 1 hits since the release of "Bodak Yellow." But she left an indelible mark on the summer of 2017, not only because she rewrote history, but she gave hope to the have nots, the people who were too scared to dream because they were repeatedly told no.

"Bodak' just brought people together," says J. White. "That was our 'We Are the World.'"[9]

As of March of 2023, "Bodak Yellow" is certified 13x platinum and counting.

It would take the entire word count of this book to list all the records it has broken.

[9]https://www.billboard.com/music/music-news/cardi-b-bodak-yellow-songs-that-defined-the-decade-8543874/

5

Be Careful

"When me and my husband got into our issues—you know, he cheated and everything—and I decided to stay with him and work together with him, a lot of people were so mad at me; a lot of women felt disappointed in me," Cardi explains. "But it's real-life shit. If you love somebody and you stop being with them, and you're depressed and social media is telling you not to talk to that person because he cheated, you're not really happy on the inside until you have the conversation. Then, if you get back with them, it's like, how could you? You let all of us down."[1]
—Cardi B, *Vogue* magazine

An unreturned hotel key.

Lipstick on a collar.

[1]https://www.vogue.com/article/cardi-b-cover-january-2020

The lingering whiff of a "fragrance" you know is not your own.

A hidden little black book.

A call that rings too late one night.

Multiple pagers.

A secret credit card.

Multiple cell phones.

A secret email account.

The Ashley Madison hack.

Bitches in your mentions.

Hints of infidelity may have changed over time, but it has remained a primary subject of popular music since its earliest inception. Whether you are looking for a song about being cheated on, or being a cheater, there are limitless titles for you to choose from.

Cheating is also immune to genre.

One would think given classic cheating titles like "Your Cheatin Heart," "Jolene," and contemporary titles like Carrie Underwood's scorcher "Before He Cheats" that there is an entire stereotype about country music being music about cheating, it would be the king of the cheating or "Cheatin' Songs."

It is in fact Hip-Hop, a relatively young musical genre, that claims the most tracks about infidelity. And we are fortunate enough to be able to say so definitively because in March of 2019 two students, Cassandra Alexopoulos, from the University of Massachusetts, Boston, and Laramie D Taylor from the University of California, Davis, released a study titled *Easy Listening? An Analysis of Infidelity in Top Pop, Hip Hop, and Country Song Lyrics over 25 Years.*

The study's introduction reads:

> Although it has been established that sexual content is common in popular music, the extent to which this content references cheating behaviors is unclear. Given the prevalence of infidelity among Americans, it is important to examine how infidelity is portrayed in media targeted to young adult listeners. To explore these portrayals, we conducted a content analysis of the 1,500 most popular pop, Hip Hop, and country songs in the United States over a 25-year period examining the frequency and nature of infidelity in music. Findings revealed that infidelity was discussed in approximately 15% of popular music, and was most frequently discussed in Hip Hop songs. Both negative and positive consequences to infidelity were depicted, and were most often accompanied by a nonchalant emotional tone.

Historically, themes of infidelity date back to the very beginning of the Blues woman as a musical force. Both Ma Rainey and Bessie Smith would strike on the theme of infidelity in their earliest works.

As noted by Angela Davis in her seminal work, *Blues Legacies and Black Feminism,* women of the 1920s would have been one of the first as Black American women to experience infidelity as we know it in modern terms, as enslavement only a generation before had precluded the ability to choose one's own sexual partners. Davis notes that "Sovereignty in sexual matters marked an important divide between life during slavery and life after emancipation";[2] additionally, "Industrial capitalization becomes the sphere of personal love and domestic confluence in domestic life. The Historical African American vision of individual sexual love linked it inextricably with possibilities of social freedom in the economic and political realms."[3]

For the next 100 years women would sing about men who stray.

Aretha was one of a "Chain of Fools" and throughout the 1950s. In the 1960s you can hear women bemoan lovers who are unfaithful but they can't leave. Given that women were not yet equal in the workforce there were economic consequences to leaving an unfaithful man. The US Department of Labor estimates:

> In 1950 about one in three women participated in the labor force. By 1998, nearly three of every five women of working age were in the labor force. Among women aged 16 and over, the labor force participation rate was 33.9 percent in 1950, compared with 59.8 percent in 1998.[4]

[2]*Blues Legacies and Black Feminism.*
[3]Ibid.
[4]https://www.bls.gov/opub/ted/2000/feb/wk3/art03.htm

As women's economic status changed in the 1970s and many states ratified the ERA, pop music saw a rise in empowerment anthems like Gloria Gaynor's "I Will Survive" that resonated not only musically, but because women could literally financially survive being left. From Angela Bassett in *Waiting to Exhale* stuffing her faithless husband's designer suits in his BMW and setting it all ablaze without a glance behind her, to the very real tribulations of TLC's Lisa "Left Eye" Lopes who famously burned her Atlanta Falcons boyfriend's mansion to the ground upon hearing he had … ummm … creeped—by the turn of the twentieth century, not only was it acceptable to part with a man who was unfaithful, you quite literally burnt it all down behind you as a symbol of empowerment.

Cardi references TLC as a double entendre, the musical act and as a playful verb when she accuses her lover of cheating. Cardi will again reference Lopes on "Thru Your Phone," another track wrapped up in the perils of infidelity where upon discovering her lover's betrayal she ponders taking things to the "Left Eye" level. The "burn it to the ground" mentality regarding cheating would be the pop culture default well into the 2010, and cross genres with Carrie Underwood's aforementioned "Before He Cheats" where her appetite for destruction stops just shy of flames.

The trend would continue until 2016 when Beyoncé released *Lemonade*.

Rumors regarding infidelity plagued Jay-Z and Beyoncé's marriage from its onset. In 2014, footage leaked of an elevator ride post Met Gala showing the Queen B frozen and her sister, Solange, who physically confronts her husband, a security guard eventually separating them, seeming to confirm something was not right in Hip-Hop's *Camelot*.

The swirl would continue until April 23, 2016, when Beyoncé would settle the matter via a visual album originally dropping on HBO. The term "cultural shift" has come to be overused, but *Lemonade*[5] was a cultural shift.

Prince had died only days before, leaving a stunned world hungry for powerfully transcendent Black music, and Beyoncé delivered. Each track is a journey through the couple's separation and eventual reconciliation by the end of which the cultural absolute of leaving a cheating man has shifted. It's hard to believe in the environment prior to *Lemonade* Cardi would not have received even more backlash for taking Offset back at all. The path of reconciliation via music was one less explored and is now on the thematic table with Bey and Jay as a template.[6]

"Be Careful," marks a moment on *Invasion of Privacy* where vulnerability, pop sensibility, and Bad Bitch R&B meet, showcasing a softer side of Cardi.

She creates a sing-a-long track for broken-hearted bad girls. It would go on to inspire "It's not a threat. It's a warning." tattoos on clavicles across the world.

---

[5]There are numerous options for academic and journalistic takes on/about Beyonce's *Lemonade*. I recommend listening to Dissect Podcast's (Spotify) phenomenal track by track episode breakdown. It's truly a thorough examination of *Lemonade*'s historical references, musicality, and cultural influence.

[6]Jay-Z would address his own issues in *4:44*, a *Lemonade* for bros, released Jun. 20, 2017.

Though Cardi attests the song was in development years before her relationship with Offset, the album's release and news of their split would naturally prompt assumptions. She begins the song bemoaning the state of her current relationship, noting it's more Tommy and Kiesha from the 1990s film *Belly* than the seemingly perfect relationship between Steph and Ayesha Curry she aspires to. Throughout the song Cardi will harden her language in situations where she is most vulnerable, in a form of musical overcompensation, as she emotionally barters with someone she knows can't fully let her guard down.

Cardi has referred to herself as both "the Trap Selena" and "the Strip Club Mariah Carey," and you can hear the influence of both women in the song's DNA.

She invokes Selena making the most of her accent to play with her delivery and weaves Spanish into her lyrics. Latin rhythm propels the track forward as she flows between rapping and singing.

She could cheat too, but she's too good to do it. She warns her man these random bar hoes he is embarrassing her with will steal his jewelry. She throws up a verbal caution sign repeatedly, insisting she is sincere.

Mariah, who spoke with Cardi for the Warhol-founded, celebrity on celebrity bible, *Interview Magazine,* asked for more songs like "Be Careful" on the next record.

Mama Mariah's presence on "Be Careful" takes notes from her infidelity anthem "Shake It Off." It is of similar tempo and thematically on point. Carey learns of her lover's infidelity, informs his mother, packs her diamonds, tosses her designer duds in her LV bags, and takes his car onto bigger and better things. The magic of "Shake It Off" is Carey's vocal prowess. The track is based on a very catchy but repetitive single beat. Then it's Mariah, on Mariah, on Mariah. A layer of her creating whoops, a layer with her repeating the song's chorus, and vocal runs all over the lead line.

The accompanying video to "Be Careful" plays with the song's light and dark duality. Cardi first comes to us visually as a platinum "Like a Virgin" bride, and later as the story turns, a scorned Rihanna redhead in widow's black, her looks serving as a visual marker to both sides of the dysfunctional relationship she is singing about. The desolate Southwestern church where the video is set goes from being warm and hopeful to cold with an intentionally isolating, clever lighting plays. The guests in the church remain throughout, like they know how it's going to end, witnessing the ups and downs of this doomed relationship.

Producers Frank Dukes, Boi-1da, and Vinylz bring a trifecta of premium samples. Most prominently that of Lauren Hill's "Ex-Factor," which pulls from Wu-Tang's "It Was All So Simple Then," and buoys its romantic sentiment in the Streisand standard "The Way We Were." Hill's endorsement of the track was noted by Cardi in an interview with Ebro Darden with *Beats 1*:

> Nobody could talk shit about this record to me because the sensei approved it.[7]

In a review for *Pitchfork*'s Track Review section critic Briana Younger said "Be Careful" was:

[7]https://pitchfork.com/news/cardi-b-says-be-careful-isnt-about-offset/

A risky, if not altogether divisive, song to drop just one week ahead of her highly anticipated debut record, *Invasion of Privacy*. It's a single that suggests the album will further reveal one of music's most accessible stars. On the other hand, for fans ready for stomp-somebody-out floor-fillers, Cardi instead has chosen refinement. She sands her edges with some laid-back raps and diffident singing over Bossa nova-tinged production. Her Latina roots are on full display and her accent more apparent than ever as she laments her significant other's inability to act right, complete with a nod to Lauryn Hill's "Ex-Factor." She's vulnerable here, but far from weak. Lines like, "You got me lookin' in the mirror different/Thinkin' I'm flawed because you inconsistent," cut to the heart of how a lover's indiscretions can mess with the self-image of even the most confident people.[8]

By 2020, Cardi herself would serve as the model of keeping a relationship together to the next generation of girls when she agreed to let a voicemail sent to hard R&B songstress Summer Walker become the outro to the opening track "Bitter" on her record *Still Over It*.

Rumors were swirling that DJ London, Walker's collaborative and romantic partner, had strayed … and she was pregnant. Cardi directly addressed the rumors and advised Walker to go at the women in her mentions and DMs, to feel free to strike back with authority and go for the verbal kill—that she is financially and professionally successful in her own right—and to express what is happening

---

[8]https://pitchfork.com/reviews/tracks/cardi-b-be-careful/

through her music and control her own narrative. Ending the conversation and call with the authoritative advice and with great emphasis on each word to "Fuck." "These." "Hoes."

"Be Careful" would earn Cardi a nomination for Best Rap Performance at the 61st Grammys. It would spend twenty weeks on the *Billboard* Top 100.

6

Best Life

I'm rooting for everybody Black.
—Issa Rae, *2017 Emmy Awards*

Just as the South Bronx can claim the title of the birthplace of Hip-Hop,[1] home of Sugar Hill Records, and Cardi B, it would also become the home of two terms that would come to be definitively important in music, culture, and the intersectionality of modern feminism in the 2010s: "Hip Hop Feminism" and "Black Girl Magic."

Joan Morgan is an Island girl, born in Jamaica and raised in the neighborhood Cardi would later call home. Her career began as a pioneer in feminist, Hip-Hop journalism and she became an awarded scholar bringing the subject to academia. Her 1999 book *When Chickenheads Come Home to Roost: My Life as a Hip Hop Feminist* is an exploration of the states of both feminism and Hip-Hop in the late

---

[1] See Chapter "I Like It."

twentieth century touching on all the contradictions of loving an art form that doesn't always respect you. It will become an often-referenced classic.

2014

Inspired by Morgan's work in 2014, model turned DJ turned mogul/mentor Beverly Bond would trademark "Black Girl Magic."

By 2016, it would become a mantra.

Available on coffee mugs, tote bags, and t-shirts, the highly meme-able phrase would also precede an unprecedented run of Black women in Hip-Hop and pop culture collectively, not only monopolizing the charts, but making artistic advances for culture as a whole.

While Cardi is dancing and hosting and finding her audience on social media, the indie scene had its first taste of internet boosted, crossover success when Detroit's Dej Loaf's "Try Me" broke the Hot 100.

The commercial success of Iggy Azalea's "Fancy" hitting number one was a landmark but muddied in Macklemore. Nicki Minaj continued her run with the radio-friendly "Super Bass," but it was Azealia Banks and her debut *Broke with Expensive Taste* that would shake up Rap and music in general.

Banks already had an aggressive and edgy flow and an even more aggressive and edgy persona. She smartly looked to Rihanna and found European Dance producers to help her carve out her sonic lane. Her eclectic sound exploration in dance music not to mention her frequently "too open" social media presence are integral to Cardi's creation. It's hard to see a path to *Invasion of Privacy* without Banks.

With Azalea and Banks in the mix, publications from *Vogue* to *Entertainment Weekly* to *Faze* to *HipHopDX* all wrote articles and headlines questioning or asserting that 2014 was "the year of the female rapper" because there were enough to count on one hand.

2015

Emerging from the corners of the internet and smaller labels, Jungle Pussy and Lizzo get their first tastes of media attention in 2015. Online publications were starting to give more coverage to these emerging emcees and conversations around the "One Queen of Rap Theory[2]" are becoming more common in the blogosphere.

"Super Bass" is still propelling Nicki Minaj onto the charts.

Cardi is joining the cast of Love and Hip-Hop and is writing her mixtape debut *Gangsta Bitch Music Volume 1*.

Beyoncé plays the 2015 VMA behind a sparkling gigantic sign reading FEMINIST sparking controversy. It was the first time she had taken an overtly political stance on stage and it set off a wave of media debates and endless think pieces hailing her as the movement's savior or its demise. What she

[2]https://thatgrapejuice.net/2015/10/female-Hip Hop-removing-the-one-rapper-rules-rule/

did was shift the conversation and claim space in it for Black femme artists that we would see build momentum and play out over the next four years.

As for whether Beyoncé's art and personal politics were about to merge, she would keep them all guessing until April of 2016 …

2016

Between 2010 and 2016 most femme rappers aside from Nicki Minaj were categorized as "indie." Which is accurate as most all were on labels that are considered Independent. Despite the myriad of declarations in 2014 about the "year of the female rappers" they are still not being signed. As we'll discuss in Chapter 13, there are reasons major Hip-Hop labels aren't stepping up.

2016 would see Black Girl Magic translated in almost all other aspects of the music charts however. Rihanna's *Anti* went hit for hit for hit changing the sonic landscape with tracks like "Desperado" and "Needed Me."

Rhiannon Gibbons would break through the prevalently pasty genre of folk with *Freedom Highway*.

Notably, rapper Noname's *Telefone* and Kamaiyah's *A Good Night in the Ghetto* make strides into the mainstream.

It was however the Knowles sisters who would like Venus and Serena before them, vie for the title, in this case "Record of the Year" with critics split between Beyoncé's confessional *Lemonade* and Solange's *Seat at the Table* as 2016's top musical offering.

Smaller labels are making investments in Femme Rap and the number of women getting coverage by the music press explodes. *LA Weekly* runs the headline "Here's How Much Women Ran Hip Hop in 2016,"[3] publication after publication starts to write up indie acts and the list is full of artists playing in widely different corners of Rap and all over the world. Chicago's Noname, Dreezy, and Tink. Cerebral Brit Lil Simz is making waves, and Young MA blows everyone away with her "Butch Thug" flow and willingness to be open about her sexuality, which only a few years prior would have made her come up impossible.

Cardi is right on time. The year 2016 sees her making the list of "Best New Rappers for Elle Magazine[4]" and first real coverage by the music press.

DJ Booth, in response to the 2016 election that set American women back fifty years, listed Cardi as one of the "Top 10 Nastiest Women in Hip Hop."

As hindsight is 20/20, one can take this then true observation comically:

"Cardi B is neither critically heralded nor explicitly political, but she spits with a confidence that evokes *Hardcore*-era Lil' Kim and makes me proud to be a woman in my own skin."

In 2016 Cardi might not have been critically heralded or explicitly political, but by 2017 she would be both.

---

[3]https://www.laweekly.com/heres-how-much-women-ran-Hip Hop-in-2016/
[4]https://www.elle.com/culture/music/a40289/best-new-female-rappers/

2017

The year 2017's list of top critical picks would include SZA's highly influential *CTRL*, Kehlani's *Sweet Sexy Savage*, Jamila Woods's *Heaven*, Sharon Jones and The Dap Kings' *Soul of a Woman*, and Valarie June's *The Order of Time*.

Despite the rising tide of femme rappers streaming well and making their mark, there were only three signed to major labels.

Then came "Bodak Yellow."

"2017 reminded us women in Hip Hop deserve their spot on the throne" declared *The Grio*.[5]

The piece by writer George M. Johnson is an example of how men often lean into femme competition as an easy form of analysis, but does a good job of describing Cardi's impact on 2017, noting:

> By May, rivalry tensions grew deeper as BET announced the nominees for Best Female Hip Hop Artist, including Minaj, Remy, Missy Elliot, Young M.A, and Cardi B.
>
> At the time, Cardi B was still fresh off her fame of Love and Hip Hop, just looking for a chance.
>
> The Bronx native self-released two mixtapes within six months of each other in 2016 and 2017. The projects proved how serious she was about her transition into music, and demonstrated she had the talent to do so.[6]

[5]https://thegrio.com/2017/12/31/2017-female-rappers-Hip Hop/
[6]It's worth finding both Johnson and Collins essays. They are exemplary examples of how men and women write about the same topics in music differently.

Remy Ma ultimately dethroned Minaj, winning the Best Female Rapper category, and more importantly broke her winning streak. It was quite the moment in Hip-Hop, as it seemed the women's rap scene finally had some healthy competition. The moment, however, was quickly overshadowed by Cardi's Cinderella come up story.

The rapper's breakout hit, "Bodak Yellow," instantly made her a bonafide star and someone to watch in Hip-Hop. Cardi had listeners shouting lyrics like "I don't dance now, I make money moves," and she most certainly made moves this year. The single quickly climbed the charts, ultimately hitting the *Billboard* Hot 100's Top 10 within eight weeks of its release, with a shot of reaching number one—a feat that even Minaj had not acquired in over eighty attempts.

On Sept. 23, "Bodak Yellow" finally did what seemed to be impossible, becoming only the second solo number one by a female rapper in *Billboard*'s history.

Not surprisingly, a woman was able to write about the same topic without the "there can be only one" mentality.

For *Vice*,[7] Hattie Collins wrote in a lovely and nuanced piece titled "2017 was the year the female rapper got the respect that she deserves."

Cardi B has of course been the stand out this year, not only managing to shatter records but deliver what is arguably

---

[7]https://i-d.vice.com/en/article/a3nvqp/2017-was-the-year-the-female-rapper-got-the-respect-she-deserved

the song of 2017. She has graced the NYT Magazine and Rolling Stone, built an insanely committed online fanbase and is currently readying her debut album. It looks like 2018 will be an even bigger and better year for the Bronx rapper—there's something particularly serendipitous that the woman breaking rap records is from the birthplace of Hip Hop. Also, Cardi did this outside of the co-sign; she didn't need to rely on a male to approve her place within Hip Hop.

It could be reductive to suggest 2017 is the year of the female rapper when we of course hope 2018, 2019, 2020 and beyond will keep female rappers front and centre of the Hip Hop canon. We'd also like to see more women in the Missy Elliot mould—women that produce music (shout out engineer K Lee) as well as rhyme. But it feels like real and meaningful headway has been made this year. Whether new names or old, underground or platinum sellers, the female voice finally rang out loud this year— she is a rapper, hear her roar.

2018

2018 was a 12 month long victory lap for Cardi B.
—Shea Serrano, *NO Skips* podcast.

By 2018, the prevalence of women in rap was so substantial that *Vibe* was able to give a Top 25 list of records by female rappers a year-end list of their own.

Some of the year's outstanding titles included Cupcakke's *Ephorize*, Esperanza Spaulding's *12 Little Spells*, The Carters'

Everything Is Love, Tierra Whack's *Whack World*, Megan Thee Stallion's *Tina Snow*, Kali Uchis's *Isolation*, Janelle Monae's *Dirty Computer*, LeiKeli47's *Acrylic*, Noname's *Room 25*, Georgia Anne Muldrow's *Overload*, Rico Nasty's *Nasty*, Saweetie's *High Maintenance*, Nenah Cherry's *Broken Politics*, and City Girls' *Period*.

And of course the Number 1 Record of the Year as declared by *RINGER, Time,* and *Rolling Stone* magazine: Cardi B's *Invasion of Privacy*.

Several online publications took to making year-end lists about Cardi's absolute domination. It was a massive enough undertaking that they, and Shea from *No Skips* podcast, went month to month with Cardi's accomplishments. As the scope of that year is so huge, it's the right approach.

January of 2018 sees Cardi featured on the Bruno Mars "Finesse Remix." It would make her the first woman with five top ten singles on the chart at once. She attends both *American Music Awards* and *Grammys* where she is nominated for "Bodak Yellow."

April is a huge month for Cardi.

Invasion of Privacy drops on the 6th, on the 7th she plays *Saturday Night Live* and reveals her pregnancy. On the 9th she became the first woman to co-host *The Tonight Show*. On the 15th she brings down the house at Coachella. On April 18 she charmed Ellen Degeranges on her daytime talk show. On the 29th she performed at the Latin Music Awards. The month will see her become the woman who broke the record for streams on iTunes and see every song on *Invasion of Privacy* chart on the Hot 100. By May she is winning the Met Gala in custom Moschino by Jeremy Scott.

July makes her the first female rapper to hit number one twice when "I Like It" tops the charts, and a mom when she welcomes Kulture. In August she has the coveted opening performance slot at the MTV Music Awards where she is twelve times nominated and will take home three awards.

In September, in a move that is equal parts Bronx Bad Bitch and pure Shakespeare, she throws her Louboutin at Nicki Minaj during New York Fashion Week and the thud is heard round the world. The incident would set the rappers up for years of beef in verse and print.

During the global pandemic when Minaj would wade into conspiracy theories regarding COVID-19, one Twitter user drily shaded "The shoe has landed."

Cardi also gets her own shade of deep, velvet blue, Tom Ford lipstick.

In October Cardi turns twenty-six and releases the stand alone single "Money."

November sees her Fashion Nova colab and reality TV show *Rhythm & Flow* drop.

In December she is one of *Time* magazine's People of the Year, nominated for five Grammy Awards (including album of the year) and "Bodak Yellow" surpasses one billion YouTube streams.

*****

"Best Life" features Chicago's Chance the Rapper and is the only track on *Invasion of Privacy* where a male vocalist takes the lead.

Chance enters sing-song-ing the song's title and goes into his verse that is also the chorus. It is also unlike the rest of the tracks in that Cardi's vulnerability is showcased outside the context of romantic love. She lists things she has been physically and emotionally insecure about and counts her blessings. There is an optimistic tone to the record, its flow could be described as a "mosey." It takes its time and in some ways is the most out of place track on a record colored with intense emotion, musically and lyrically. You can see where the later released single "Money" may have been more at home mid-record.

Cardi's second verse tells us where she has been and where she is going and notes her meeting Beyoncé and Tina Knowles as a milestone moment and a flex on the other girls. Meeting Bey is one thing, getting the attention of Ms. Tina, designer extraordinaire, "The Blueprint" and the platinum uterus that brought us both Solange and Beyoncé means something else. She tells us she is the flower that breaks through pavement ala Tupac's *Rose from the Concrete* in its physical form.

The track is short. Producers Boi-1da and Allen Ritter keep the production light throughout and "Best Life" serves as a positive, palette cleanser and gives a grateful Cardi a chance to express it.

7

I Like It

"There's no hood harder than my hood," the "Bodak Yellow"
singer, who became the first rapper to have three songs
break the Billboard Hot 100's Top 10 list last month,
tells i-D Magazine.
Though the breakout artist is clearly making "money
moves," she's not above looking back on her early years in
the city … I wouldn't be able to rap about the things that
I rap about now [if I hadn't grown up there].[1]
—*AM New York*

Where we can call "Get Up Ten" a lyrical origin story, "I Like
It" is a musical one.

Within the track we can hear Cardi's multicultural
background. It serves as a respectful nod to the neighborhood
she grew up calling home, to the place that is home of Latin-
inspired break beats, and music that is colored with a vivid,
island palette that reflects in the neighbors island flags and
local graffiti.

[1]https://www.amny.com/entertainment/cardi-b-bronx-1-16718403/

The track spans generations with trap beats intermingling with an unmistakable Boogaloo hook. The song's accompanying video shot in Miami's Little Havana makes for an audiovisual melting pot where Afro, Latin, and Caribbean music intercede.

Between 1970 and 1975 the Bronx became the first New York City borough with a majority Black and Latino population.[2] In the midst of this demographic shift, 1973, it would not coincidentally also be the birthplace of Hip-Hop.

In the summer of 1973 Roe v Wade was months old. The war in Vietnam is in "suspension." The first meeting of The National Black Feminist Organization is about to occur, Nixon is about to resign and a wholly American art form is about to be born when on August 11,[3] as the *Bronx Times* puts it:

> It was there at Highbridge's 1520 Sedgwick Avenue that an 18-year-old Jamaican immigrant by the name of Clive "DJ Kool Herc" Campbell invented a new genre of music when he looped the break of James Brown's "Give It Up or Turnit Loose" inside of the packed rec-room.

It would be the second time the neighborhood would take part in multicultural, musical fusion to form a new style of music. The late 1940s and early 1950s had seen a massive migration of Caribbean immigrants to NYC and the Bronx in particular. In the early 1960s, the neighborhood would,

---

[2]https://www.nytimes.com/1976/04/19/archives/blacks-and-puerto-ricans-a-bronx-majority-study-finds-blacks-and.html
[3]https://www.bxtimes.com/a-history-of-Hip Hop-in-the-boogie-down-bronx/

along with its upper borough brethren birth Latin Boogaloo, a fusion of soulful R&B rhythms and Latin-based beats, like mambo.

Of the booming Latino population in 1970 New York, 70 percent of Hispanics in New York City were of Puerto Rican descent with the vast majority of these immigrants settling in the Bronx. The second highest settling group in the Bronx would be of Dominican descent. The 1970s would see the area economically depleted, undersupported by the City, and by 1980 the neighborhood was a burned out shell of its former self and its residents in daily peril. Yet throughout this, Latinos in the Bronx would contribute greatly to putting the Boogie in what would become known as the "The Boogie Down" Bronx.

The University of Michigan Online explored the history of Latinos in Hip-Hop on the academic level in which they accessed:

Although it is widely acknowledged that Hip Hop began in the early 1970s in the South Bronx, New York, the mainstream media view it as an African American cultural expression. African American tend to view it as exclusively their own, and even Puerto Ricans and other Latinos tend to view it as "black" music. However, its birth and development were a joint creative effort of African American and Latino Afro Caribbean youngsters, particularly, Puerto Ricans …

Hip Hop began as an expression of poverty—stricken inner city minority youths who grew up during the 1960s and 1970s. It is a musical form that incorporates a shared, lived urban experience that revolves around music-rhyming and dancing; often makes a social statement against the harsh realities they must deal with on a daily basis; and graffiti. While African Americans concentrated on serving as disc jockeys and master of ceremonies, Puerto Ricans and other Latino Caribbeans contributed heavily to the hip hop aspects of breakdancing and graffiti.[4]

Sharice Davis for *Vibe* magazine quoted Hip-Hop scholar George Nelson in a piece titled "Why Latinos Can't Be Left out of the Hip Hop Narrative" supports the university's thesis.

While Hip Hop has been heralded as an inherent creation of the African-American community, the art form is equally tied to its Latino roots. "[If] you talk to Grandmaster Flash, Kool Herc, or Afrika Bambaataa or any of the early DJs they all talk about the breakers, who in the '70s and '80s were mainly Latinos, and keeping them happy on the dance floor," Hip Hop historian Nelson George writes in Latina.

According to the pop culture expert, the essential role Latinos played in writing the Hip Hop narrative is hard to ignore considering they pioneered the revered core element of breakdancing. "If you talk about some of the famous break crews who really broke through and got known by the early '80s, the majority were Latino dancers

[4]http://websites.umich.edu/~ac213/student_projects06/student_projects/lhh/images/notes.html

like Rock Steady Crew's Crazy Legs," he continues. "So if the idea of the Hip Hop DJ is predicated on keeping dancers dancing, then the Latino aspect is crucial. Their aesthetic, their taste, their ability to dance, all affected what was played and how it was played."[5]

When Cardi began her performance rapping "Bodak Yellow" in Spanish on her *SNL* debut it was a marked moment. She chose on her largest national stage to date to announce her Latina heritage upfront. There had been a few Latin and Latin American artists to play the show, the first being Desi Arnaz in February of 1976. It would be 2022 before *People* magazine could announce:

> Rosalía performed twice on Saturday's show, treating the audience to "Chicken Teriyaki" and "La Fama." She is now the first woman to perform both songs entirely in Spanish in the NBC sketch comedy series' 47-season history.[6]

Rosalía made her SNL debut in a guest spot three years prior. Her first time on the show was to perform with Bad Bunny in 2019.

One of two Latin guest artists featured on "I Like It," the track would mark the Puerto Rican rappers (born Benito Antonio Martínez Ocasio) first appearance on the American Top 40 charts. A year after "I Like It" catapults Bad Bunny in to North American consciousness he lands his own *SNL* slot.

---

[5]https://www.vibe.com/features/viva/why-latinos-cant-be-left-out-of-the-Hip Hop-narrative-445344/
[6]Rosalía Performs 2 Songs Fully in Spanish in Her Solo Return to "Saturday Night Live"—Watch!

By 2022 he would not only find success in American cinema, he would become Spotify's most streamed artist globally.

Merging the musical worlds between Reggaetón and Latin Trap, J Balvin, the track's second featured artist, was an explosively successful interactional artist prior to "I Like it." A Grammy Award winner, the Colombian Reggaetón sensation had hit the ground in 2014 and quickly became one of the biggest selling Latin artists of all time, and the first to secure headliner status at large US festivals like Coachella.

*****

There is a reason *Rolling Stone* declared "I Like It" their number 11 in the list of greatest "Summer Songs of All Time:"

In the summer of 2018, it was nearly impossible to stand on any street corner in any American city without hearing "I Like It" blasting from the window of a passing car. "I Like It" was where Cardi B really gave it up to her Latin heritage, with Puerto Rican rapper Bad Bunny and Colombian reggaetón star J Balvin, over a trapped-out sample of Pete Rodriguez's 1967 boogaloo classic "I Like It Like That." While Cardi hits the timbale beat like a piñata, she gives the guests room to shine—this has to be the first Number One hit in history to namecheck Celia Cruz, Jimmy Snuka, and Lady Gaga in the same verse.[7]

[7]https://www.rollingstone.com/music/music-lists/best-summer-songs-of-all-time-43407/hot-fun-in-the-summertime-sly-the-family-stone-83290/

"I Like It," as a song is not here to play. From the jump it hits you with a sample everyone knows. It instantly drops you and Cardi back in the musical heart of the Bronx, referencing a track from her borough brethren that would help birth breakbeats, Pete Rodriguez and immediately spins it, almost literally into Latin Trap. Cardi's delivery hits with the same attention-grabbing force. Her focused and pointed enunciation turn a list of things she likes—dollars, diamonds, stunting, shining, and million dollar deals into a tight flow without an overt rhyme scheme.

To say the track was created in expert hands would be an understatement. Chairman of *Atlantic Records* Craig Kallman, who had success as a producer in his own right, brought the Pete Rodriguez sample to "Bodak Yellow" producer J. White Did It. It would take over seven months and several locations to make the song, the international hit it became. In an oral history of the song for *Billboard* magazine they discussed finding the magic:

Kallman: Once in a while, I'll go back to my DJ roots like when I produced the Lupe Fiasco "Daydreamin" record with Jill Scott which won a Grammy. That was the last record I produced to be honest. I thought I'd retire on that one, but Cardi inspired me to dust myself off. I have about 1.1 million vinyl albums, so I went back to digging in the crates. I used to DJ in NYC and used to play any genre of music. I was known to be the DJ that no matter what night it was, German Krautrock, salsa, punk rock. I had the biggest record collection. I have this Latin music collection and pored through it and put together hundreds of sample ideas. Pete Rodriguez was always one of my favorite artists. "I Like It Like That" and "Oh That's Nice" are two of my favorite records. I always felt like that could come back as an idea. The Blackout Allstars had done it as a dance record. I started in my bedroom with it, moved it to my own recording studio and starting looping up the samples. At that point, I needed a collaborator on the beat and started experimenting.

J White: I go to Craig's house and he said he felt like he could split a Latino record. He thought it'd be big for her, the culture and the industry. I'm like "Wow, that's a great idea." Literally, I'm on no sleep, I'm tired, it's 12:00 at night. Craig is talking to me about all of this and I'm half sleeping, I'm dozing off. He's like, "J White, I'm going to play through some records." By maybe the ninth record, I'm about to be at his house asleep. I heard the "Yeahhh, baby! I like it like that!" and I said, "Ah!"

Kallman: This record had the most obvious hook and one you could base the chorus around. The other samples were meant to be woven.

J White: Anytime you feel a record, anytime you feel anything like that in your system, in your bones. That was my Starbucks. I was ready to knock it out.[8]

It would take two more producers, brought in by Edgar Machucha director of A&R for Atalanitc, whose relationships with Global Latino artists help him attain his position.

[8]https://www.billboard.com/music/latin/cardi-b-i-like-it-oral-history-8471835/

Machucha first turned to Tainy, a huge Reggeaton producer who J. White Did It credits for making the song "grow into its chorus."[9] After months of work, they decided to bring in producer Invisible Beats who worked from LA while the rest of team toiled in Atlanta. Described by Machucha as his "secret weapon," Invisible Beats added live instrumentation and sample recreation, notably from Pete Rodriguez "Oh That's Nice" layered in.

When she was invited to perform at the 2018 American Music Awards she chose the song to punctuate what would be her historic night. Much like the songs video they lean in to bright fashion and colors and left no one in doubt that she loves and revers her Latina and island roots.

"I Like It" proved Cardi the rare crossover artist who can export American Rap comfortably in Spanish. Cardi's ability to tap the Latin Music market and Hispanic purchasing power, a multibillion dollar industry, is an instrumental part of her global success.

After the success of "I Like It," Cardi would go on to another Latin collaboration with Ozuna and Selena Gomez. The track, "Taki Taki" produced by DJ Snake, would see Cardi in September of 2018 becoming the first female rapper to occupy the top of Spotify's Global Chart.

[9]Ibid.

8

Ring

The duet, a musical composition where two musicians (known as a sonata) or vocalists (known as a cantata) contribute equitably to the performance, is cemented in popular music. Mozart is credited with bringing instrumental duets to popularity as he, from childhood, wrote duets for himself and his sister. Vocal duets gained particular notoriety in the genre of opera, where lyrical delivery serves as the story's principle dialogue.

Opera would also provide women their first opportunity for high earnings via the arts, though American opera would remain an almost exclusively white space until the New York Opera Company offered a contract to Camilla Williams. A Virginia native and soaring Soprano, Williams would go on tour internationally, find prestige in Fine Arts academia, and to sing the Star Spangled Banner before Martin Luther King, Jr. Gave his "I Have a Dream" speech.[1]

[1] https://www.washingtonpost.com/entertainment/music/camilla-williams-an-acclaimed-soprano-who-broke-racial-bounds-dies-at-92/2012/01/30/gIQA0QfedQ_story.html

Groups of women singing together often found success in the early days of *Billboard*. The chart was founded in 1958 and the Shirelles became the first girl group to hit #1 with "Will You Love Me Tomorrow" by January of 1961. And though a wave of other girls in groups would soar through the sixties, it wasn't until 1979 when superstars Barbra Streisand and Donna Summer teamed up for "No More Tears (Enough Is Enough)" that two women held on to the position together on the same track.

Streisand was one of the world's top-selling artists when they recorded together, but it was the Summer of Donna in 1979. In April she had dropped "Bad Girls," and by June of that year she hit number one. A few weeks later she would take up the number two and three slots of the first female top five, which was almost exclusively disco and Black with the exception of Rickie Lee Jones's "Chuck E's in Love." Sister Sledge with "We Are Family" and Anita Ward and her Bell at number one. It was no wonder Streisand sought to get herself "Moroder-ed" too.

It would be almost twenty years before two women would hit #1 together again. They would go on to hold the honor of longest running female duet for over twenty-two years and be the first Black women to do so together. Brandy and Monica, two 1990s babies and R&B divas paired in 1998 for "The Boy Is Mine" which held on to the *Billboard* Hot 100 top spot for thirteen weeks. While the track is a simple one that thematically fails the Bechdel Test,[2] it gives both vocalists ample opportunity to show their individual range and sweet,

[2]https://www.merriam-webster.com/dictionary/Bechdel%20Test

teen harmonies. In a piece for *Buzzfeed News* writer Michael Blackmon gives background on the seminal track:

> Brandy and Monica, who were 18 and 17 at the time, hadn't actually met before they recorded "The Boy Is Mine" in 1997. The idea to come together was originally Brandy's, who was hoping to quell the persistent rumors that the two teenagers loathed each other. "We're friends and we're cool and no matter what anybody says we're going to stay tight," said Brandy in a late-'90s interview clip about the collaboration. Monica, while promoting her second studio album, The Boy Is Mine, on Live with Regis and Kathie Lee in '98, also seemed to suggest they were on the same page. "When we did the song together, [there] were all these misconceptions about controversy, but I think it kind of took the fun out of it for people to see we got along," she said. Still, this act of resistance proved futile as the wildly popular pop stars' budding relationship inevitably became frayed. Though adept at singing, the two were not at all prepared to endure the manufactured rivalry that seemingly became a real thing. Ironically, the duet won the pair a Grammy Award for Best R&B Performance by a Duo or Group in 1999, a shared honor that remains the only Grammy each of them have to their name.

Into the new millennia, duets and collabs conquered the pop charts. Critic Jody Rosen posed in 2006 if duets had "peaked" citing the year's prevalence:

> Rapper-singer and rapper-rapper collaborations are ubiquitous, and these songs overturn the long-standing

verities about duets. They're typically arranged marriages, orchestrated by record companies as a kind of pop music product placement. In most cases, the artists scarcely communicate—they quite literally perform different songs, with disparate musical texture and lyrical content. And yet, the songs often work. Hip Hop duets have been around for decades, of course. Rappers have been teaming up with each other from the beginning, and when it became clear, sometime around the early '90s, that Hip Hop was here to stay, singers began drafting rappers to add a little gruffness and street credibility to their songs. (The deal worked both ways: MCs who might otherwise have been embarrassed to sing love songs felt free to explore their sweeter, softer sides when sharing a track with an R&B singer.)[3]

Female collaborations were not part of the seeming 2006 renaissance however.

From 1991 to 2011, the Grammys celebrated Hip-Hip duos and groups as individuals. Over the categories' ten-year span only Salt-n-Pepa and Lil' Kim's remixed "Not Tonight" would see women nominated.

In 2011, Rihanna remixed with Britney Spears on the even sexier "S&M Remix" and Aussie Iggy Azalea and Brit Charlie XCX hit with "Fancy" in 2014.

It would take six years, but as noted in a piece by Heran Mamo for *Billboard* on June 2020 they note that "Out of the eight female duets that reached No. 1 on the Billboard Hot 100, three of them made history in 2020 alone" and also

[3]After clip, https://slate.com/culture/2006/11/how-the-duethas-conqueredthe charts.html

On May 16, (2020) Doja Cat's "Say So" remix featuring Nicki Minaj earned both artists their first No. 1 hit. In that week's tight race for the top spot, Megan Thee Stallion and fellow Houston powerhouse Beyoncé debuted at No. 2 for the Megan's "Savage" remix, a historic move where four black female soloists occupied the No. 1 and No. 2 positions on the Hot 100.[4]

Mamo's piece also mentioned the success of Lady Gaga and Ariana Grande's 2020 "Rain on Me" saying it was

a pivotal year for Ariana Grande, who notched her record-breaking fourth No. 1 song with Lady Gaga's Chromatica single "Rain on Me" that the Little Monsters and Arianators showered with praise. Grande became the first artist with four No. 1 debuts, following her and Justin Bieber's "Stuck with U" quarantine anthem from May 23, "7 Rings" from February 2019, and "Thank U, Next" from November 2018.

It was with listeners ears that were primed for female voices particularly of the Hip-Hop variety that a mere three months after Mamo noted the trend, Megan Thee Stallion and Cardi would release the biggest female duet of all time and the first to debut at number one: "WAP."

"WAP" not only shattered records but taboos, and the societal shift prompted by the song will be studied by music and social scholars as long as we study both.

The track also served to elevate Cardi, as well as Megan, to superstar status shared by the likes of Gaga, Beyoncé,

[4]https://www.billboard.com/music/pop/favorite-female-duet-no-1-hot-100-poll-9404485/

and Rihanna. The single would see Cardi tie Grande's record. "Up," released a year later, would see her break it.

The biggest legacy of "WAP" may be that it prompted the industry to finally move femme-fronted collaborators to the forefront of twenty-first-century music. Whereas Cardi primarily started as a featured artist on the tracks of male acts, post "WAP" we see her collab with and bring up primarily with women and nonbinary artists, including duets with other women of color like Lizzo, Normandi, Rosalía, and GloRilla, and collabs with R&B baddies Summer Walker and SZA. The latter of whom first appears with Cardi on one of the two duets with women[5] on *Invasion of Privacy*, the album's final track, "I Do."

The first is "Ring" with versatile Oakland artist Kehlani who once, in song, boastfully yet aptly described herself as the love child of Aaliyah and Tupac.

An outstanding vocalist and rapper, their 2014 self-released mix tape parlayed them into a deal with Atlantic Records. Naomi Zeichner at The *Fader* magazine, in a 2015 piece on Kehlani noted they were part of a new artist classification called "mindie."

> Kehlani pays her rent with money from her label, Atlantic, which is priming her as a crown-jewel "mindie" act—a major artist with indie bonafides. Now that streaming has become more popular and grassroots Vine memes have started breaking actual hits, it's an increasingly common strategy. A label provides studio time and marketing budgets to an artist who has already found some success

[5]Kehlani began using gender neutral pronouns in 2018.

independently, taking care not to disturb the existing (and profitable) direct relationship the artist has with their fans. In some cases, these partnerships are kept quiet so fans don't feel like their favorites have changed course; for example, the rapper Logic has said he worked with Def Jam well before announcing his deal.[6]

Cardi would also sign with Atlantic after the release of *Gansta Bitch Music I & II*. You can see how the "mindie" strategy would be perfected by the time it was applied to the 2017 launching "Bodak Yellow" as a single and subsequently *Invasion of Privacy*. Through social media and reality TV, Cardi was able to have a readied audience much larger than other "mindie" artists before her but was able to capitalize on the structures being in place for her larger success.

Label mates have often been paired in duets by record companies in hopes of not only a hit single, but a bump to the catalogs of both artists involved. Sometimes it can feel contrived as Rosen mentions above, but in-house musical couplings often create great art and label success, even when it's personally messy—think Terrell, Gaye, and Motown.

Pairing Kahlani and Cardi, both Atlantic artists with crossover audience appeal, while merging their respective styles on the track was a smart play for all involved.

"Ring" rolls in as a low key R&B jam. Kehlani debuts the song's hook, soulfully bemoaning how long it's been since her lover reached out. A crisp high cat fixes itself on the top of the Needlz and Scribz Riley mix while a soft popping drum line

[6]https://www.thefader.com/2015/08/04/kehlani-cover-story-interview

holds down the bottom. Cardi raps her way onto the track cleverly suggesting other body parts her MIA man could use instead of his seemingly broken texting thumb. Throughout the song she flows between rapping and occasionally singing. The vocal play is used to put emphasis on the highs and lows of the emotional roller coaster that is being left on "read" too long.

The song's video is fairly standard for artists launching at their level. It's shot on a set. The outfits are coordinated to exactly match. A blonde Cardi and Kehlani are steeped in old communication technology like rotary phones and isolated, lonely, floating phone booths invoking the very twentieth-century feeling of endlessly and hopelessly waiting by a stationary phone for it to ring. Director Mike Ho goes so far as to wrap Cardi in literal phone cable, to drive the point home even harder.

The song would be the final of the album's five singles, debuting at number #28 on *Billboard*'s Top 100, giving Kehlani her first taste of Top 40 magic.

9

Money Bag

> How many times do you have to leave your purse in your
> dressing room and have it go missing before you say I
> worked hard for this money? I'm going to put my purse
> right here where I can see it.
> —Rickey Minor

Aretha Louise Franklin (or simply, Aretha, as she is
universally known) was born March 25, 1942.

Crowned the "Queen of Soul," she will, until there is no
longer a form of recorded music, be instantly recognizable
for her powerful delivery and chill-inducing vocals.

When asked to define her religion in the famous Prost
Questionnaire, folk singer Marianne Faithfull put it
succinctly: "Aretha Franklin is the voice of God."

Her career, from its beginnings at twelve in her father's
traveling Gospel show to her final appearance in November
of 2017 at the age of seventy-five, would be heralded as one of
the greatest of all time. The mention of her name alone, one
of the first women in popular music to be so famous she need

only be addressed in the singular, instantly conveys what you should feel when you experience music at its best.

New York Magazine's fashion blog *The Cut* noted Chanel and Louis Vuitton[1] as favorites and that her bags were always designer. When she died, some headlines focused on her legacy, while many focused on the story of Aretha and her famous purses.

Coordinated with Franklin's luxurious furs and embellished gowns, her ever fabulous bags were more functional than a flex.

Aretha Franklin. The voice of God. The Queen of Soul, known throughout the world and forever by her first name only, had to carry her purse on stage and keep it in her sight line, because no one around her could be trusted not to steal from her.

In a piece for the *New York Times* esteemed music critic Gavin Edwards[2] recounts Aretha's performance of "Natural Woman" performance at the Kennedy Center. The piece is a group conversation with several of the key players in the production of the event. The conversation soon turns to Aretha's purse, which became an expected part of her stage attire. Glen Weiss, executive producer and director of the Kennedy Center Honors ceremony recounted:

> She always walks onstage with her purse. When we were in rehearsals, she walks out and puts it on the piano. When she walks downstage, she picks it up and puts it

[1]https://www.thecut.com/2018/08/aretha-franklin-purse-ode.html
[2]When Aretha Franklin Brought Down the House at the Kennedy Center, Gavin Edwards, Aug. 16, 2018.

on the floor. The show ends with everyone in the tribute downstage signing "I Feel the Earth Move." In rehearsal, there's a line of people in street clothes—her, James Taylor, Sara Bareilles, Janelle Monae—and this one bag sitting in the middle of the stage. When we finished James Taylor leaned forward to pick up the bag and hand it to her, being a gentleman, and reflexivity she almost pushed him away.

Rickey Minor, Musical Director of the Kennedy Center Honors ceremony continued:

The purse thing has a long history: she has to keep her money on her at all times. She's got her money, she's ready to move, to go wherever she needs to be. How many times do you have to leave your purse in your dressing room and have it go missing before you say I worked hard for this money— I'm going to put my purse right here where I can see it?[3]

So it is out of good taste, disrespect, and financial necessity that Aretha Franklin invents the proverbial "Money Bag."

Unfortunately, Aretha is only one of countless Black women that have been robbed literally and figuratively in the history of popular music.

Danyel Smith, author of the sublime *Shine Bright: A Very Personal History of Pop Music*, recounts Soul legend Mahalia Jackson[4] carrying her cash, sometimes nearly $20,000,[5] in her ample bra for the same purpose.

---

[3]Ibid.
[4]Smith, Danyel. *Shine Bright: A Very Personal History of Black Women in Popular Music.* USA: Roc Lit 101/Penguin Random House, 2022.
[5]$20,000 in 1920 is equivalent in purchasing power to about $296,171 in 2020.

Shirley (Pixley) Goodman was only thirteen when she co-wrote what would become a musical standard "Let the Good Times Roll" as half of Shirley and Lee. The duo who were promoted as "the sweetheart of the blues" who may or may not have been a couple in their early teens[6] quickly became so popular they spawned imposter touring acts.[7] Goodman however would not be adequately compensated until she was nearly sixty years old after years of suing the estate of her partner Leonard Lee. Continuing to work, though sporadically, into the 1970s Goodman would intercede with Hip-Hops inception when she and future Sugar Hill Records founder Sylvia Robinson paired up on the pre-disco era, dance single "Shame, Shame, Shame."

Donna Summer, another Queen of her genre, had to sue Casablanca Records for her fair share of the profits from her earth-shattering Disco hits, a style of music she helped define.

Women of color navigating the perils of financial success in the music business dates to its inception with the likes of Ma Rainey and Bessie Smith whose respective work at the beginning of the twentieth century would see them become pioneers in approaching femme-fronted music as a business, and attempting to control their own financial future.

Musical archivist Chris Albertson recounts:

Bessie rose to become the highest paid Black entertainer of her day, with earnings totaling $2,000 a week. That was a mere pittance by today's standards, but it was

---

[6]Tricia Diamond, source for our chapter discussion on twerking, is a relative of Goodman. The family version of the story is that the couple dated briefly as teens but were then promoted as a couple.

[7]https://www.womeninrockproject.org/reference/goodman-shirley/

considered a small fortune in the twenties, especially in the netherworld of Black show business, which Bessie embraced. And though she had to pay the show's salaries and expenses out of that money, the amount she could claim as personal profit was a staggering one for a woman who grew up in abject poverty.[8]

Almost one century after Bessie Smith netted $96,000 per year, making her one of the highest paid Black women in show business, Cardi B's net worth (in 2022) was estimated at 40 million dollars.[9]

For all of Cardi's well-earned success, the wage gap for the average Black woman in 2022 was around 64 cents for every dollar earned by her white male counterparts,[10] so it would make sense that Pussy Rap as a niche genre would become centered on the acquisition of wealth and an "any means necessary" approach to financial security.

Why play by the rules when the deck is so stacked against you? If women aren't able to earn the equivalent of their male counterparts, getting a bag, whether it be a designer bag or a stacked bag of cash, or both aka "the full Aretha", shouldn't be a surprising concept. If you have to work nearly twice as hard to get yours, the idea you should be in his bag, even if you have your own, makes sense.

Not only subject to the wage gap, we can also attribute Westernized standards of beauty like long, straight hair or

[8]Chris Albertson. "Bessie Smith: The Complete Recordings Vol. 1." *Liner Notes.* https://www.thecut.com/2018/08/aretha-franklin-purse-ode.html
[9]https://wealthygorilla.com/cardi-b-net-worth/
[10]*Business Insider*, April, https://www.businessinsider.com/gender-wage-pay-gap-charts-2017-3

surgically exaggerated body parts that have been deemed "ideal" and cost thousands of dollars to maintain, to the Black femme financial burden.

Extensions or a good wig, lashes, contacts, facial skincare, full even lips, hairless underarms, body skin care, moisture, moisture, moisture, perfectly symmetrical breasts, an exaggerated tiny waist, nails so good they shame other women, hairless nether regions, more moisture, moisture, moisture, a huge ass and proportional thighs that match, hairless legs, toes pedicured to perfection, and if you are wearing anything at all it better be Bottegas.

Even if you took on half these practices, and some women take on all of it, the calculated time and expense are staggering. And that's before you're clothed.

Pussy Rap as an art form recognizes Black women are earning nearly half what white guys are, but are asked to bear additional economic burdens of beauty and femmes are right to demand their worth be recognized.

As Cardi's contemporary and "WAP" counterpart Megan Thee Stallion put it on her witty retort to Kayne West's "Gold Digger," "Sugar Baby" she reverses the stereotypes portrayed in West song down to musically reversing the memorable hook of "Gold Digger": "You can't have opinions on shit you ain't paying for."

If the cost of being valued and loved is equated with these costly "necessities" why not expect the inequitable expense to be shared?

Once a main topic of a male-dominated genre, "Gold Digging" has now become gender neutral thanks to the new generation of Pussy Rappers.

You'll find frequent references to contraception and safe sex throughout the genre often equated with economic consequences of motherhood, flipping the gold digger stereotype on its head. Their rhymes boast of their own personal wealth making them targets "for getting trapped" with children, popping Plan B, an ovulation blocker, so as to not be stuck with any man they see as inferior, and affording them many jokes about keeping men for oral sex only (also known as "a munch" or "an eater").

After all, if you have managed to subvert systemic patriarchal capitalism's attempt to keep you down, i.e., park a custom orange, $300,000 Bentley across a marble rendition of Versace's famous Medusa, why should you settle for anything less than the very best head?

The quickest way to the Bentley? Your name on a bag, whether it's designer or McDonald's brand collaborations have quickly become a big, big bag for femme rappers.

They have become more important, not only as a means of clout and access to the best in high fashion, but because streaming money is meager in comparison to what an artist would make from record sales in the past.

Fortunately by 2020 female rappers would be the most in demand celebrity collaborators. *Culture Shift* an online music blog noted:

While women in Hip Hop have been dominating the global charts (and headlines) for decades, marketable ambassadorship roles have historically been reserved for a different breed of celebrity—mostly white, mostly actresses or pop singers and mostly with a squeaky-clean public record. In the last few years, notable improvements to this lack of inclusive representation have been made (Rihanna for Dior, Beyoncé for Adidas) but 2020 has seen a more palpable shift in the push for brand diversity. This year, three multi-million pound companies tapped some of the most successful women in rap (Cardi B, Megan Thee Stallion, and Saweetie respectively), to represent their businesses at a global scale. A move that not only celebrates the commercially-successful careers of these female rappers but also openly recognizes the power of their international influence.[11]

Cardi's first collaboration would come with shoe retailer Steve Madden whom she told *Teen Vogue* she chose because:

All of this came about because I keep bringing up to my manager, I want to work with brands that are affordable. And are chic but good quality. I don't want to work with a brand that is like, "Yeah they make shoes," or "Yeah, they make clothes," but it's like … cheap, not good to wear. I've always been a fan of Steven Madden. We have a mutual friend, and bam! We connected.[12]

Next would come two collections with Fashion Nova the first of which sold out all eighty-two pieces within minutes,[13] the second collection as reported by *Refinery29* reporting on *TMZ*, reporting on Cardi.

[11]https://cultureshiftuk.com/female-rappers-2020-brand-ambassadors
[12]https://www.teenvogue.com/story/cardi-b-fashion-nova-collection-million-launch
[13]https://www.vox.com/the-goods/2018/11/15/18097465/cardi-b-fashion-nova-instagram-influencers-clothing-collection

TMZ is reporting that the second Fashion Nova collection from Kulture's Mom sold out completely within 24 hours of its launch last Friday. She made the company $1 million on the first day of sales alone, which totally outperformed her first collaboration with Fashion Nova. The initial offering launched in November 2018 and sold out almost instantly. So you could say that all Fashion Nova sees is money (heh).[14]

By 2023 she would expand into athletic wear in collections with Reebok and other branding deals with McDonald's, Rap Snacks, and Whip Shots (a blend of alcohol and whipped cream in a spray can) which seems by all accounts to be a fine product, but makes the following quote a bit hilarious:

A lot of people that don't like me used to be like, "Oh, nobody will ever take her serious, nobody will ever sign her." And it's like, if only y'all knew. People are dying to sign me, I just … if the numbers ain't right, I won't settle for less. I feel like I deserve a lot because I know what I could bring to the table. I could sell anything. I could sell ass in a can.[15]

*****

"Money Bag" takes what could be a variety trap song and saturates us in the best of the subgenre. Cardi chants the song's title then "woos" her way into the track as it clicks in with a punctuated crispy high hat and a pointed digi synth

[14]https://www.refinery29.com/en-us/2019/05/232611/cardi-b-second-fashion-nova-collab
[15]https://www.thefader.com/2017/06/22/cardi-b-atlantic-records-deal-contract

line that holds for a four count before bringing in a blown out, warbling bass drum line and sped up Trap style, triple-timed, hi-hat just as Cardi drops her list of the luxury cars she will be driving this week to the beat. The established time signatures and her repetition of the phrase "money bag" and various "woos" hold throughout the track, providing a steady bed for Cardi to list the ways looking like a "Money Bag" and getting a Money Bag are intertwined all while throwing in some very trademark "skurrrts" "yeahs" and "yelps."

Producers Laquan Green and J. White Did It aren't afraid to drench us in Cardi, giving vocals layer on top of vocal layer and long, intentional, echo bleeds that bounce all over the mix. Cardi and Pardison Fontaine (aka Jordan Thorpe) get playful with their glammy and sexy lyrics, using the song to compare how much Cardi differs from the women stereotypically depicted in Trap music. While she's making millions she points out other hoes are at "the stove." Just in case you'd like to challenge her, she is also quick to mention she travels with a bevy of lethal, identical beauties ready to remind you their roots are gang, and then questions how you can perform oral sex and talk shit about her at the same time. Karas Lamb of *Entertainment Weekly* in their review of *Invasion of Privacy* states the importance of "Money Bag" writing that she is "Fending off the trolls in her mentions who predicted she was out of gas after 'Bodak Yellow'" and that "Appropriately, 'Money Bag' eviscerates detractors who have tried to play her cheap."[16]

---

[16]https://ew.com/music/2018/04/09/cardi-b-invasion-of-privacy-review/

10

Bartier Cardi

What is the female gaze, then? It's emotional and intimate.
It sees people as people. It seeks to empathize rather than
to objectify. (Or not.) It's respectful, it's technical, it hasn't
had a chance to develop, it tells the truth, it involves
physical work, it's feminine and unashamed, it's part of
an old-fashioned gender binary, it should be studied
and developed, it should be destroyed, it will save us,
it will hold us back.
—Tori Telfer, *Vulture.*[1]

We open on a glistening swimming shot through a cloudy
lens, purposely distorted. It's a transportive haze that feels like
it might be part memory. It's warm and feels disassociated.
It is highly erotic and makes you feel like at any minute a
very hot femme could show up with a very open top and a
very empty pizza box ala a vintage porno.

[1]https://www.vulture.com/2018/08/how-do-we-define-the-female-gaze-in-2018.html

A pair of long legs come into frame and swish a net through a suburban-esque backyard pool where it becomes apparent there is a lot of cash afloat. The camera pans up another pair of legs attached to a striking, dark-skinned woman perched poolside. The picture being painted is pure, pastel grindhouse. The kind of thing Quentin Tarantino might conceive of if he weren't being misdirected by his penis.

There is but a moment to take in this seductively languid criminality, before Cardi appears in a flash cut. Her mouth strikes the camera. Then we are back to our quite literal sexy, sexy money laundering.

A receptionist flanked by big bills smears a finger through a bowl of dip on her desk. As she licks her fingers we see another babe come into view running a cash through a money-counting machine. It's old school. The kind you'd see the back room of a Mobster flick.

We pan back to the gorgeous Black girl stirring money through the pool and blip back to Cardi, who is in a platinum wig, part Mae West, part Lil' Kim in "Lady Marmalade" clad in red satin lingerie and big diamonds in a celebration of big, bawdy, hyper-femininity.

The grandiose persona, honed by West, was rife for Hip-Hop pillaging. A New Yorker and pro-sex feminist light years ahead of her time, West would become famous for her great comedic timing and one of a kind delivery. She came up in Brooklyn, in the era where burlesque and vaudeville would collide. Her combination of humor, sexuality, and physicality would be emulated throughout the years including by a young Janet Jackson whose impression of West brings her to the public consciousness. Lil' Kim, another Broooklynite pro-sex feminist with great delivery who was years ahead of her time, would declare herself "the Rap Mae West" on her verse in the all-star track with Missy Elliot, Angie Martinez, and Left Eye, "Not Tonight."

The "Not Tonight" video features a slew of well-oiled men in subservient positions with a technicolor and tropical feel. The "Bartier Cardi" video will also feature well-oiled men, but director Petra Collins sullies the sheen, making for grittier context.

Collins's trademark is a type of light play that produces a softening effect on her subjects you could call almost frangible as it makes for dreamlike images. And while it's something that we have become accustomed to in a world of fast filters, when Collins began her career as a teenager in the early aughts the look was singular. Her work is self-described as "Fueled by self-discovery and a contemporary femininity which explore the complex intersection of life as a young woman online and off."[2]

She is the perfect choice to introduce *Invasion of Privacy* as a visual concept. The video features an online assortment of Instagram influencers as employees of Madam Cardi who had been shooting themselves in Collins's signature style for years. She spoke about social media and intense femme scrutiny:

> I recently read a random article about Kim Kardashian and her Instagram and I think it made a really good point about this. It goes back to how people are allowed to

[2]https://petra-collins.com/cv/

enjoy looking at a woman's body, but she's not personally allowed to enjoy it herself. As soon as she starts to feel good and proud in her natural state, society punishes her. It's this weird push and pull and so confusing to girls as they grow up. It's like you can be sexy, but you can't be sexual, you have to be submissive, but also in control, and you have to be beautiful, but you can't show what goes on behind the scenes.[3]

Much progress in feminist art was made in the 1970s. Cinema was no exception. French Filmmaker Chantel Akerman, whose *Jeanne Dielman,23, qui du Commerce, 1080* is often credited for bringing the female gaze to prominence. She recalled bringing the European idea to America.

In the early 1970s when I arrived in New York from Paris, there definitely was the desire to invent a female gaze. Women started to shoot films made by women and also for women. We all felt that men had shown their point of view since the beginning of the world and we now should try to find if we could invent a new language that would be different from the one of our fathers or lovers.[4]

Feminist scholar Laura Mulvey's 1975 work *Visual Pleasure and Narrative Cinema* brings the term "The Male Gaze" as a

[3]https://crfashionbook.com/fashion-a9541895-petra-collins-photography-feminism/#:~:text=Petra%20Collins%20Leads%20a%20New,Through%20Photography%20%2D%20CR%20Fashion%20Book&text=As%20a%20photographer%2C%20an%20artist,inhabits%20more%20roles%20than%20most.on%20behind%20the%20scenes.#%E2%80%9D
[4]https://www.vulture.com/2018/08/how-do-we-define-the-female-gaze-in-2018.html

concept into prominence. Through the initial essay and book of the same name she deconstructs the concept and its place in the patriarchy of cinema.[5]

Black women like Carrie Mae Weems were also exploring the intimacies of womanhood with honesty in images both still and moving.

Weems, a trained photographer and dancer, studied Folklore at Berkeley and you can see the feminine storytelling tradition in her work down to her often-emulated use of light. Critic bell hooks was a champion of Weems's photography declaring

> [Her] photoworks create a cartography of experience wherein race, gender, and class identity converge, fuse, and mix so as to disrupt and deconstruct simple notions of subjectivity.[6]

*****

"Bartier Cardi" features a guest appearance from 21 Savage. If you're familiar with his catalog, his contribution is standard fare "He's fasting so no pussy, thanks."

Collins chooses to subvert the misogyny of the verse with the imagery. As he raps, Savage is progressively bound by two tall Black women. They are not gentle. It's purposefully left unclear whether he is being punished or rewarded.

---

[5]https://www.perlego.com/knowledge/study-guides/what-is-laura-mulveys-male-gaze-theory/
[6]https://hyperallergic.com/700735/bell-hooks-left-behind-a-legacy-of-scholarship-on-art-and-love/

The video marks what will become a trademark for Cardi's video work. If you review her catalog, Cardi is never shot in a position that is submissive to a man. Even when she is in scenes with Offset she is on top, physically.

Like most pop femmes before her, Cardi adapts personas, sometimes in the multiple. In "Bartier Cardi" we will see the first inkling of her "Arty" Cardi persona. Once well-honed, it will be Cardi at her most Gaga and Grace Jones.

It's not just visual; Arty Cardi has a specific sound. It's music that's not necessarily her poppiest work. It's her most subversive. She leans into her weirdness. We'll hear it musically again on the record with "I Do" and later in her post *IoP* catalog with "Money," and "Press."

The track comes in with a simulated organ grind. Producers 30 Roc and Cheeze Beatz lean into the eerie arc and drop a spinning hit hat and trappy bass drum. Light keys punctuate the Cardi verses and hold the melody. It's meant to throw you off kilter and it's very effective.

Collins's direction would be recognized in 2018 when the video was nominated for Hip-Hop video of the year at the 2018 MTV Video Music Awards.

"Bartier Cardi" is the second video from *Invasion of Privacy*. Cardi announced on Twitter that she had spent 15,000 dollars out of pocket on the video for "Bodak Yellow," the single that predated the album. It's not surprising "Bartier Cardi" features several product placements to offset production costs. She seductively plays with an Eos lip balm, makes out with Offset in a branded LYFT, and retailer Fashion Nova has their name everywhere. It marks Cardi's selling power and her taking control of her financial agency.

Though it had a place at its inception, the term "female" gaze is currently not broad enough to cover the entire identity spectrum. In 2019, *Dazed Digital* writer Aimee Cliff noted in a piece titled "How the music videos of the 2010s saw women take back power: From Rihanna's revenge fantasy to Lady Gaga's surrealist pop vignettes, the male gaze of the 00s was subverted" and notes that it was queer directors moving the needle forward.

As we move into the 2020s, there's a sense that the old template has been ripped up. The next frontier is being led by queer women—if the 2010s explicitly resisted and subverted the male-on-female gaze, the 2020s is poised to ask, why so heteronormative? While queer sexuality in pop music videos in the 00s was generally played for men's approval (think TATU, or Britney and Madonna), the 2010s has, very gradually, moved towards a more inclusive vision of female sexuality thanks to the likes of Hayley Kiyoko, Halsey, Shura, and Christine and the Queens (who unquestionably made the sexiest video of 2019 with Charli XCX in "Gone").

By 2010, it was passé to make a video that catered to a man who sat and watched a woman dancing. By 2020, it feels like it's also become pretty passé to make a video that subverts or comments on that old trope. In the 2020s, the stage is set for women to make pop ever more adventurous and ever weirder, hopefully leaving the male gaze ever further behind like the dusty, ancient relic it should be.[7]

[7]https://www.dazeddigital.com/music/article/47263/1/rihanna-beyonce-christina-aguilera-music-videos-male-gaze-2010s

The main subject of Cliff's piece is none of the celebrities she mentions. She rightfully credits director Melina Matsoukas, a queer, Black woman as one of the forerunners in this visual change. Her early work with Beyoncé in 2007 led to a decade-long streak shooting the most powerful women in pop. Her subsequent work on Bey's *Lemonade* would move the medium, and the female gaze forward in the broader public's consciousness.

The trend would extend to social media as young femmes on Tik-Tok began conversations around subverting the male gaze through fashion. A new generation of femmes are conscious of gender perceptions on film from an early age.

The *Daily Utah Chronicle*[8] documented the trend:

> "I only ever found my personal style when I stopped dressing for male validation and the male gaze because it was boring," TikTok creator @lilrotini comments in her video, with over 285 thousand users liking in agreement. The fashion stylist Arabella breaks down her past fashion choices and explains how she consciously dressed for a male audience, wearing "things that would show my body off, but they never were really cool."
>
> In the sea of videos following this trend, users' appearances for male validation have some key visual similarities. Outfits are very simple, form-fitting and grace a muted, pastel color palate. Users typically wore minimal

---

[8]https://dailyutahchronicle.com/2021/09/04/tiktok-trend-female-gaze-gender-expression/

layers in favor of high-waisted pants with a cropped shirt combo. T-shirts are often V-neck, makeup is simple and feminine and boldness is avoided.

Beyond the visual cues of the male gaze, intention also plays a big role in its definition. "The goal was for people to say, 'She's so hot!' not [to use] my platform to express myself," comments user @lexie_jayy. For her, the intention behind her appearance was what connected her to the male gaze and not necessarily what she was wearing.

"Even though I'm still wearing a micro mini dress it's not giving, 'Oh my god, can I be your girlfriend?' It's giving 'bad b*tch,'" she said in reference to her most recent outfit choices. Lexie makes an important discovery—the trend frames a narrative that clothes equate to gender and that certain articles pertain to certain perspectives. This mindset can be extremely harmful, and it's important to remember that clothes are simply clothes, and that ideologies rest in intentions.

11

She Bad

Oh My God, Becky, look at her BUTT! It's sooo big. She must
be one of those "Rap Guys" girlfriends, "Baby Got Back"
—Sir Mix-a-Lot

The Venus of Willendorf is thought to be around 25,000
years old, making it one of the first art forms known to
man. Most scholars agree that Venus of Willendorf is a
"Mother Goddess," a deity that appears in almost every
known religious sect. The Venus of Willendorf and her
Venus "Sisters" discovered through the 1920s, they are given
the name of the Roman goddess through worldhistory.org
explains:

> The term Venus figurine is used to describe the more than
> 200 small statuettes of voluptuous female figures that have
> been found at Upper Paleolithic sites across Europe and
> some parts of Asia. 'When paleoanthropologists refer to
> figures as Venus, [they] usually do so with air quotes' (von
> Petzinger, 95), because Venus figurines pre-date myths

about the goddess Venus by thousands of years. The name is derived, in part, from theories that associate these figurines with fertility and sexuality, two traits associated with the Roman goddess.

A "Mother Goddess" is a creator ripe with fertility and is often portrayed as mother earth. She can also be a destroyer laying waste to all she bore.

As mentioned above, the Venus figures earn their names due to their "voluptuousness."

The Venus has a full belly and breasts to remind us she brings life. Her hips are wide and of the birthing variety. And it's abundantly apparent, from the front, what she has behind her, is ass. And a lot of it.

An exaggerated, rounded, peach-shaped backside has in the 2020s become a sought-after standard of beauty. The case is easily made that the cosmetic procedure known as a BBL is one based in cultural appropriation, where Black women's bodies that have been historically hypersexualized for their curviness, are now being replicated by non-Black women.

For those unfamiliar, *Dazed Digital* in their "Brief History of the Brazilian Buttlift" defines the BBL procedure:

> Buttock augmentation is the surgical process of altering the size, shape, and contour of the buttocks. This can be achieved using silicone implants or fat transfer, what's commonly known as the Brazilian butt lift. BBL surgery begins with liposuction to remove unwanted fat from one area of the body (stomach, flanks, and/or thighs).

The fat is processed and then reinjected into the buttocks to improve contour.[1]

It's also the cosmetic procedure with the highest mortality rate. The buttock has the body's largest blood vessels and can carry a mis-injected mass of fat directly to the heart or brain.

White women like *Mad Men's* Christina Hendricks and Kim Kardashian—who along with her family would sell waist trainers to create the illusion of a "snatched" waist and larger posterior—would help mainstream embracing of the bigger backside. Now you will find BBLs hotly debated on Twitter and various online forums. Girls will discuss whether they should invest in a car, or an education, or a BBL? The majority of the replies all seem to be that the right BBL will have someone paying for your car/education. The refrain of "shake what your mama gave ya" has been replaced by "what ya doctor gave ya" and the girlies aren't looking back.

As a young stripper, Cardi recounted the pressure to live up to this newly enacted ideal undergoing a back alley augmentation different and more dangerous from a traditional more expensive BBL as recounted by GQ in 2018:

> She wanted fat for her ass because (1) her boyfriend had recently cheated on her with a woman who, per Cardi, "had a fat, big ass" and (2) she'd observed that her colleagues with big asses made more money than she did stripping, regardless of dancing technique.

[1]https://www.dazeddigital.com/beauty/article/46497/1/brazilian-butt-lift-plastic-surgery-kim-kardashian-west-cardi-b-jennifer-lopez

Cardi claimed her ass from the universe in a basement apartment in Queens, where, for $800, a woman injected her buttocks with filler. "They don't numb your ass with anything," she says. "It was the craziest pain ever. I felt like I was gonna pass out. I felt a little dizzy. And it leaks for, like, five days."

The circumference of the final product cannot be determined beforehand, which makes this procedure risky even among illegal medical procedures. While Cardi was happy with hers, she planned to return for a touch-up. "But by the time I was gonna go get it, the lady got locked up 'cause she supposedly killed somebody. Well"—Cardi clarifies with c'est la vie insouciance—"somebody died on her table."[2]

For women who predated Cardi's career in popular music, physical standards of beauty were different. Narrow hips, long legs, flat torsos, and protruding breasts that can be seen from the side were considered the ideal through much of the 1960s through to the early aughts. The standard was defined by whiteness as these characteristics were "ideal" because they were more often present on European, white bodies.

Hip-Hop sees the rebirth of celebrated backsides. This shouldn't be surprising as you can find the origins of ass in popular music throughout the inception of the Blues where numerous songs mention a "big legged woman" as an ideal and female singers boasting about their generous size.

---

[2]https://www.gq.com/story/cardi-b-invasion-of-privacy-profile

MTV, being a visual media, would perpetuate thinness as an ideal, but by the 1990s generous posteriors would become more prominent in popular music. In 1990, Bell Biv Devoe would implore us to "never trust a big butt and smile" in their hit "Poison." Prince would instruct us to move our "big asses round this way," so he could work on a stressed to broken zipper in 1991's "Gett Off."

And of course in 1992, five months and four days before Belcalis Marlenis Almánzar would join the rest of humanity, Sir Mix-a-Lot dropped his ode to asses "Baby Got Back" which could arguably be the moment "big butts" started to break through the mainstream.

In 1993, Snoop Dogg would also introduce the world to the word "Bootylicious" in the track "Fuck Wit Dre Day," and Miami rapper Trina would prove to be fifteen years ahead of her time in her seminal track "Pull Over" where she defines what would become the much-lauded ideal by 2020s Pussy Rappers: To be a "10 in the face, slim in the waist" and of course "Fat in the ass."

It would, however, be three young women with roots in Houston, Texas, who would get the word added to Merriam-Webster's dictionary in 2004, as it would take over ten more years for femme culture to start to reclaim "all that ass" as body positivity and self-love as opposed to male validation of a woman's body is driving the debate, and ultimately patriarchy, marrying the concepts of fuckability and fat asses.

When Destiny's Child dropped "Bootylicious" on May 22, 2001, all three young members were conventionally slender so the anthem, while still introducing the concept of body empowerment, doesn't carry the full impact of what would become a movement. But as is often the case, barriers are broken with small cracks and "Bootylicious" with its catchy refrains proved to be an infectious one.

The ratio, the famous waist to hip standard used as a fertility metric,[3] was blown up and out of proportion with the emergence of Nicki Minaj and her overly exaggerated, Jessica Rabbit on steroids proportions. Minaj would later tell Joe Budden, Lil Wayne (who is Minaj's label head and technically her employer) would make "jokes" about her lack of ass, leading the rapper to resort to risky surgery and a re-proportioning of her body,[4] creating a standard nearly impossible to replicate.

What was once deemed "fat" is now "thick," "thique," "jelly," "cake," "Bootylicious," "healthy," or (a personal favorite) "buttered," and as these may be seen as signs of societal advance, it's through reclamation and self-love that femmes, particularly POC, have been able to remind society they are the originators of these sought-after attributes.

Though it may have been the Kardashians re-purposing of Black culture that eventually "normalizes" fat asses among white, Western beauty standards, it's Rihanna, and her brand *Fenty Savage X* that would introduce inclusive sizing and all-sized models, seeming to single-handedly bankrupt

---

[3] https://www.psypost.org/2016/10/study-finds-waist-stature-ratio-key-determinant-womens-bodily-attractiveness-45474

[4] https://soundcloud.com/joebuddenpodcast/a-conversation-with-nicki?utm_source=clipboard&utm_campaign=wtshare&utm_medium=widget&utm_content=https%253A%252F%252Fsoundcloud.com%252Fjoebuddenpodcast%252Fa-conversation-with-nicki

Victoria's Secret and their 1990s "Angel" body type. A feat that is nothing if not BAD in the very best way.

In 2022 Cardi would announce she had the majority of her "ass shots" removed:

> After I gave birth to my son, my ass was fucking huge… I almost gained 20 pounds, and that went everywhere on my body. And you know my ass already had some motherfucking ass shots. So my ass was already fucking huge as shit. Putting that baby weight on my body, plus them ass shots … a lot of people thought that as soon as I gave birth, I got my body done. No, bitch, I didn't. In August, I did surgery and I removed 95 percent of my biopolymers.
>
> It was a really crazy process, and all I'ma say is … if you young—if you 19, if you 20, if you 21—and sometimes you too skinny and you be like, "Oh my god, I don't got enough fat to put on my ass, and everything, so you resort to ass shots—don't fucking do it," she said. "I am super, super, super, super against ass shots. I'm super against biopolymers."

Beyoncé's own body would evolve with the terminology she helped bring to popularity and would find herself literally embodying the "Mother Goddess" concept in her 2017 *Grammy* performance where she channeled Oshun the Yoruban fertility goddess, the Virgin Mary, and Durga the golden Hindu mother deity.[5]

---

[5]https://qz.com/909266/the-goddesses-from-india-to-nigeria-that-beyonce-channelled-in-her-grammy-performance

She is very pregnant with twins of her own, semi-baring her full belly and breasts to remind us she brings life. Her hips are wide and of the birthing variety. And it's abundantly apparent, from the front, what she has behind her, is ass. And a lot of it.

*****

"She Bad" is track 11 (Cardi's self-professed lucky number) on *Invasion of Privacy*.

Producer DJ Mustard drops his signature "Mustard on that Beat, Ho" tagline, and his frequent collaborator, YG comes in with a chorus of "Dat Ass" (repeated ×4) "She Bad" (repeated ×4). He flows through the introduction of "She Bad" letting the listener know her ass and badness are one in the same. He goes on to list a selection of designer bags, Gucci, Fendi, Prada, Louis Vuitton, and Hermes's prized favorite, the Birkin. These valuable works of fashionable art are poised to be something attainable through a giant ass and badness.

Cardi's verse is pure bravado—she is loved by her ex and new man. Iced, rich, and feared, she is the baddest of the bad who wears the late, acclaimed designer Virgil Abloh's brand Off-White to church, and whose hotness causes the preacher to perspire.

Off-White is conscious of designing for Black bodies, but it's a rarity.

It makes sense when Cardi later bemoans she'd be more comfortable buying at curve-friendly, affordable retailer Fashion Nova because even though she can afford designer clothes, many fashion houses still refuse to design for non-sample sizes (US size 0–2) and whose shoppable collections top out at a size 8/10 when the average American woman is a size 16/18.

Her second verse goes even bolder starting with a list of bad bitch qualities, sexual boasting, designer demands … and a proclamation which would cause a social media flurry.

Cardi states she has no interest in stealing your man, she had her sights on model Chrissy Teagan (who responded to the verses in a tweet showcasing the popping eyeballs emoji) and universal, dream threesome partner Rihanna. It also notes one of the many times Cardi will mention her open bisexuality on *Invasion of Privacy*.

YG closes with the third verse in a punctuated synopsis of the first two. He reiterates she is bad and in the bag, disses accessible bag designer Dooney Burke, declaring she is Birkins only, and that she does wear Off-White to church, and is sexually fluid.

"She Bad" entered the US Singles charts at number 57 and remained for two weeks. It would go on to, like every track on *Invasion of Privacy*, to be certified platinum or higher.

12

Thru Your Phone

In 1959 Western Electric, which would come to be known as AT&T, debuted a telephone model one-third its standard household size, specifically to accommodate the bedroom nightstand. It was only a few years before that telephones were standard issue and built specially for uniformed function.

But the new model available in pink, white, blue, turquoise, ivory, and beige was a monthly add-on, and often required a bit of rewiring as most homes only had one installed jack. The compact new design boasted a slight curve, built-in illuminating dial, and a name designed to specially attract the market for which it had specifically designed. "The Princess Phone" quickly became a phenomenon.

In 1955, Philco introduced its first nonstationary phonograph. By 1959, they had become a common household device. Unlike the phone, multiple manufacturers jumped on the chance to build these compact players with a built-in speaker. The affordable, portable units came in every conceivable variety, and popularly included the same pastel-hued palette as the coveted Princess Phone.

Since we have been documenting the phenomenon of modern femme teendom, the phone and the record player, in one form or the other, have been found synonymously in their bedroom.

The rise of the mid-century middle class afforded teenagers "pocket money" for the first time. In an era of general economic affluence and a 70 percent tax on the wealthiest Americans the United States was at its most stable, allowing even lower class teens who had always worked to contribute to family the ability to keep some of their own money.

The minimum wage was around a dollar and a teenager working 15 hours a week could afford ten 45-inch singles (which averaged around 65 cents a piece) with money to spare, giving teens and particularly young women to consume pop music voraciously, and to whom musical artists were being specifically packaged, a tremendous amount of economic impact on the music business giving them ten direct votes as to who would ascend to the tops of music's newly created charts.

Middle-class homes with multiple bedrooms offered kids space to personalize with fan art and listening to music with a door closed or headphones turned that space into a universe.

A phone in their room offered teens even more freedom. Out of their parents' ear shot, they were free to practice and develop slang. The personal telephone would also give teen femmes the ability to use their voice in fandom. They could more easily organize letter and postcard campaigns in support of their favorite acts.

The Disc Jockey call-in was a staple of American radio. Wielding an enormous amount of power, on air hosts were the sole delivery system of new music. Music loving girls used their telephones to compete to request songs, win merchandise, and occasionally special access to music artists, their suggestions often compiled into nightly countdowns giving radio execs their first tastes of reliable listener data. The practice would continue through the music video era, with MTV's *Total Request Live* serving as the model at its peak.

These two technologies whose patents would be issued in close proximity run in tandem for centuries, each becoming more compact, feature-filled, and progressively interdependent would always be packaged—sometimes for just a little bit extra, because, why not?—in femme-friendly palettes, that would change music forever.

Teens with a matching pink princess phone and record player could hardly imagine that in the course of their lifetime they would be able to use voice recognition to ask their pastel pink phone to play any song in the world, at any time. It is not even something they would have seen on *The Jetsons*.

By 2018, when *Invasion of Privacy* is released, musical listening technology and the telephone will have long merged into one sole device. Had they not, Cardi, as the artist we know her as today might not exist.

Vine was created as a short video platform with easy edit controls. It's most notable features included a live view count so you could see who responded to your work in real time. The mid-aughts saw a deluge of social media platforms each competing for your content and attention. Vine's premise of watching people watching you would soon come to be standard in their competitors and finally lead to their own demise. Cardi used the platform as well as a variety of other social sites to promote both her stripping and hosting gigs. Her short clips included relationship tips, sex advice, and blunt truths all being delivered with her developing signature style. When she famously posted her clip about the ability of hoes to stay warm, perfectly coiffed in elaborate braids and dressed to slay, it might be the first version of the Cardi B persona we see today.

On YouTube you can find compilations of Cardi's social media video posts organized via platform and year. Through these short clips you can see her style, vocal presentation, and her comfort level with the camera all grow. You will also find her voicing in-depth political and sociological opinions. As she would reference in "Get Up Ten" speaking her truth was what led to her explosion of followers across all the apps available in their phone.

There have been several times and for varying circumstances that Cardi has shut down or closed her various accounts. It makes news. The hundreds of millions of collective followers across her platforms, all influenced by her posts, are a huge market for her music and the brands she represents. Each purge comes at a cost. As the breaks are often attributed to her mental health it seems to be one that is worth it. Her dedicated internet fan base or "Bardi Gang" as they are known are but one of a group of fan collectives around the internet who band together to support their artists. Sometimes for better or worse, to the extreme.

Beyoncé has the BeyHive.
Lil' Kim has the BeeHive.
Megan's fans are Hotties.

Sawattie's? Pretty Girls.
Rhianna has a whole Navy.
Lizzo fans are Lizzbians, of course.
And Nicki would be nothing without her Barbs.

The Bardi Gang is but one fan group, but their importance to Cardi's record breaking achievements cannot be understated. One of Cardi's most impressive records to date is *Invasion of Privacy* being the longest consecutive charting debut of any female rapper. That is due in much part to the collective feminist action of the Bardi Gang who use social media to directly organize streaming parties and listening times when the record was in danger of falling off the charts. Much like the girls who wrote letters and organized phone-in support for songs and videos, by the force of their sheer numbers held Cardi till she met the record and carried her over the finish line for her debut's three consecutive years on the *Billboard* Hot 200.

Excessive fandom of course has a darker side. A mob that can be weaponized for you is still a weapon, and when an internet fan base comes for you, that's exactly what it is. And while no one can be responsible for their fan base as a whole, there have been, on occasion, instances where artists were, to put it mildly, irresponsible with their power. Stan culture, unfortunately, has proven gender neutral.

There would be enough examples of the scary side of internet fandom that in 2023 Janine Nabers and Donald Glover would write a satirical black comedy about obsessive modern Fandom entitled *Swarm* where the protagonist's phone to pop star fanaticism besets her down a dark path.

As the social movements and election of 2020 showed us, collective fandom when used for good can also make positive change. When a BTS board organized to disrupt the ticketing of a certain Presidential candidate's rally, it was a youthquake heard round the world.

This is exactly the type of fanatical support that could propel a former stripper from the Bronx to number one without the typical music gatekeepers who would have frowned on her being her most authentic self.

Much like Vine before it, a short video platform resonated with kids in the 2020s. One of the most appealing aspects of the platform, TikTok was how it had integrated short music clips, whether through dance or lip-synched video, directly into the content creation process without fear of copyright infringement.

"Thru Your Phone" would not only chart upon the release of *Invasion of Privacy*, but TikTok would receive the song in short snippets, as an anthem for those feeling the sting of a lover's unfaithfulness being brutally evidentiary. Pretty girls, sad girls, tough girls, and guys too, all emoted to the visceral lyrics, making you believe they were rightfully threatening Clorox in their unfaithful boo's Cornflakes.

All Music took note of the very Cardi form of catharsis of "Thru Your Phone" in its review of *Invasion of Privacy*:

> "Thru Your Phone" is unflinching and relatable, wherein Cardi burns with vengeance as ponders poisoning her cheating man with bleach and a good, old-fashioned stabbing. It's cartoonish, but real, a confession of thoughts

that are all too familiar to the scorned. This balance between over-the-top party starters and thoughtful reflection makes Invasion of Privacy an impressive debut for a rising star who can back up her outspokenness with raw talent.[1]

"Thru Your Phone" is meant to mess with you. The song first hits you with a distorted organ riff that sounds exactly like love gone wrong. You can hear it was once pretty, but something has, to put it mildly, derailed.

If waking up to your scorned person standing over you holding your phone six inches from your face had a sound, producers Benny Blanco and Andrew Watman nail it.

Blanco was kind enough to give us some insight into the project. He got involved through Andrew Watt and his enthusiasm for Cardi led to them immediately coming up with the song's beat.

When asked what his favorite part of the song was and why?

Cardi has a tone that's unmatched. She could speak the phone book and it would sound like the coolest thing you've ever heard.

She was pregnant while she recorded the song. How does someone do that? I can't even record a verse without running out of breath. Her personality seeps through into every song she does and it leaves you begging for more.

[1] https://www.allmusic.com/album/invasion-of-privacy-mw0003166060

When asked what he was most proud of bringing to the song he modestly said: "Nothing. I'm just lucky enough to be in the room."

It's the second time on the record Cardi begins her launch verse with "Look."

The first is on "Get Up Ten," it's the first thing she says on the album.

When someone starts a conversation with "Look," you can be sure you are about to do some listening. And this time her delivery of "look" softens, but it indicates she is about to go on a long run delivery wise. She drops in at the same time as a snappy, click beat, as she contemplates telling this fool's mom about his infidelity.

The trap high-hat picks up time and so does Cardi. In seemingly one breath (and as Blanco noted, pregnant) in a bar that goes around 35 seconds she unleashes a 123-word backstory of side bitches, betrayal, contemplates the destruction of his most important possessions (his sneakers and giant TV) and invokes the name of Lisa "Left Eye" Lopes, so you know her man in real trouble.

She has been wronged "thru the phone" literally and the phone is the methodology she will use to seek revenge. She'll call your mom. She'll put the side chick's boobs on Instagram, and God help your group texting friends now that she's got receipts on them too.

Cardi will also sing on the chorus of this song with singer songwriter Alexander Tramposi. The vocals are layered. Some are more cartoonish and exaggerated than in "Be Careful," some are sweet and sad, conveying the song's emotional instability.

She does another short verse where she listens to Beyoncé's "Resentment" and chooses violence in the form of poison. She quickly reverts to her more emotional and sympathetic side. She confesses she's visualized their encounters and contemplates the safety of her health and home. She goes back to her quick cadence from the first verse, the drastic nature of thoughts spin. She ends our emotional roller coaster ride with the unsteady chorus, intentionally leaving the ending open to interpretation.

"Thru Your Phone" debuted at number 50 on the *Billboard* Hot 100 and spent three weeks on the charts. It was certified platinum on March 23, 2022.

13

I Do

Patriarchy is nimble and lithe. Its margins of operation always seem to be expanding. Feminists have naturally tended to arrange their battle lines in front of the aspect of oppression that they have regarded as the most pressing. If 'patriarchy' has returned as an idea in public debate, it is because feminism has returned with renewed vigor; because inequality has not been eradicated.[1]
—Charlotte Higgins, *The Guardian*

Sha-Rock was part of Funky 4+1
Roxanne Shante was in the Juice Crew
Queen Latifiah and Monie Love were members of Native Tongues
Lil' Kim was part of Biggie's Junior Mafia.
Trina was a protege of Trick Daddy.
Ladybug Mecca was a Digable Planet.
Lady of Rage repped Death Row.

[1]https://www.theguardian.com/news/2018/jun/22/the-age-of-patriarchy-how-an-unfashionable-idea-became-a-rallying-cry-for-feminism-today

Gangsta Boo and LeChat were affiliated with Three6 MAFIA.
Diamond and Princess were part of ATL's Crime Mob.
Mystic was given her introduction by Digital Underground.
Eve was a Ruff Ryder.
Lauren Hill was a Fugee.
Foxy Brown and Amil repped Roc Nation.
Remy Ma came to us via Terror Squad.
Yo-Yo had the co-sign of Ice Cube.
Rah Digga was a member of The Flipmode Squad.
Mia X came to you via Master P.
Nicki Minaj is team Young Money.

To say Hip-Hop is a boys club is polite. To say it's a patriarchy is accurate. The music industry has long suffered the effects of CIS gendered, straight, male gatekeeping and Rap has long upheld the male co-sign as a signifier of a femme artist's worth. It would take until the 2010s for femme artists to carve space for themselves, but by 2022 women would upset the status quo and appear to be on the cusp of dominating the game. Cardi's success as an independent artist begins a streak of femme MCs as "independent artists" breaking the standard Hip-Hop tradition of "the girl in the crew."

One of the greatest aspects of music proliferation on the internet and accessibility through social media is that it has made music industry gatekeepers less relevant. For almost its entity the music business has been owned and operated by men, mostly white, at every level. A man signed you as A&R, a man produced your record, a man did your publicity, a man decided who would get radio play, editorial coverage, shows at venues, dictated how tickets were sold, and did it in a manner that consentingly benefited themselves in the process.

For years Hip-Hop had an almost *Highlander*-type quality to women in the game. Letting only one voice predominantly dominate the space. It was the attitude of the music business in general that a singular female voice was enough. Commercial radio famously only allowed one to two women on their play rotation, meaning all women making popular music were competing for single Top 40 slots across genres for the entirety of the twentieth century.

Women were making progress in Hip-Hop but were still being under-acknowledged. NPR asked in 2014, "Where Did All the Female Rappers Go?" Critic Erik Nielson reminded folks that the late 1990s had seen great strides in women as an active Hip-Hop force, but by the early 2000s things had really devolved:

There were enough women recording, touring, and getting radio airplay that, in 2003, the Grammys took notice and created a new category for Best Female Rap Solo Performance.

Just two years later, however, that category was eliminated, with Grammy representatives citing a precipitous decline in the number of female artists in the industry who could compete for the award. BET and VH1 made similar arguments for dumping female categories from their Hip Hop awards shows as well … While cutting these awards undoubtedly exacerbated the decline in the years to follow, there's little doubt that women were indeed vanishing from mainstream Hip Hop. According to Ana DuVernay, who directed the 2010 documentary *My Mic Sounds Nice: The Truth About Women in Hip Hop*, the numbers tell it all: Whereas in the late 1980s and early 1990s there were more than 40 women signed to major labels, in 2010 there were just three.[2]

The year 2010 would denote one of the most impressive contributions to Rap by a femme artist to date.

Though she is the lone female artist, and self-noted "rookie" on Kayne West's "Monster," she is the most heralded for her performance where she outshines Rick Ross, Jay-Z, and West himself.

Cole Cuchna's *Dissect* Podcast which does deep musical dives, going track to track on seminal albums, said of her work on "Monster:"

> Nicki Minaj's verse on Monster is a masterclass in lyricism but even more so in delivery. She performs a phenomenal dynamic range of vocal peaks and valleys. Her elastic voice effortlessly fluctuating from subtly softness to diabolic crescendo like a virtuoso pianist.[3]

Minaj winds up on the track because of another woman, namely Hip-Hop paramour Amber Rose.

In July of 2022 Rose would state on The Ringer's *Higher Learning*:

[2]https://www.npr.org/sections/codeswitch/2014/03/04/285718351/where-did-all-the-female-rappers-go
[3]*Dissect* Podcast, Season 2, Episode 28.

"I had Nicki pull up to the studio and I put her on 'Monster.' She was still coming up and I saw her in the studio and I was like, 'Oh my god this bitch is fucking talented as hell,' and then I went back to Kanye and I was like, 'You need to get this girl Nicki on 'Monster,' and he was like, 'Who? What? No,'" Amber Rose recounted.

She stated Minaj's proficiency was almost left on the cutting room floor due to West's own insecurity with him asking her, "How the f*ck did you bring in a bitch that killed me on my own song?"[4]

****

Cardi voiced her opinion in an interview with Apple music when the interviewer asked how many women she had in Hip-Hop to look up to growing up as opposed to the current number in the industry.

When I was younger … about 6,7,8 there were a lot of female rappers and then there was a time when there was no female rappers at all then I had to replay the songs from the early 2000s and I had to keep replaying and replaying and replaying. And then there was one female rapper that dominated for a very long time, she still dominates. But now there is more, but you never know when there is going to be a drought.

[4]https://www.musictimes.com/articles/85953/20220721/kanye-west-vs-nicki-minaj-monster-amber-rose-explains-whos.htm

By the summer of 2017 when "Bodak Yellow" was just catching fire, the numbers for women in Rap hadn't gotten better. Almost exactly one year before *Invasion of Privacy* dropped and a few months before "Bodak Yellow" would shake the industry like a snow globe, *Pitchfork* writer Chris Mulanphy speculated in headline if the "industry would support more than one rap queen at a time" and in the piece stated:

> Simply put, the music industry has supported only a handful of platinum-level female rappers throughout Hip Hop history. One rap queen generally reigns at a time, while a handful of others hang on at a lower commercial tier. There was one particularly fertile period at the turn of the millennium where the industry supported several women rhymers concurrently, but beyond that glorious moment, the history of female rappers as sales forces is thin. And in the 21st century, it's steadily gotten worse.[5]

The online magazine also analyzed the rosters of each major Hip-Hop label and found dismal representation.

Cash Money had two, Def Jam and Rhymesayers had one, Maybach Music Group, 300 Entertainment, G.O.O.D. Music (Def Jam), Top Dog Entertainment, OVO Sound, Cinematic Music Group, Mass Appeal, ROC Nation, Dreamsville, Stones Throw Records, Fat Beats, and Mellow Music Group had zero.[6]

[5]https://pitchfork.com/thepitch/1487-will-the-mainstream-support-more-than-one-rap-queen-at-a-time-a-charts-investigation/
[6]https://pitchfork.com/thepitch/rap-label-gender-breakdown-by-the-numbers/

The heads of those labels with no female Rap representation in 2017 include Jay-Z, Drake, Kanye, Nas, J. Cole, and Rick Ross who would tell Power 105's *The Breakfast Club* that if he didn't sign female rappers because of his investment in an attractive female artist, he believed, entitled him to sex with her, stating: "You know, she looking good. I'm spending so much money on her photo shoots. I gotta fuck a couple times."[7]

It's notable that these gatekeepers are also artists who gain personal and professional advantage controlling the market and who have access, essentially dictating who they will allow to be their competition. Only allowing for one "Queen of Rap" and promoting conflict between femme artists for publicity and sales serves not only to line their pockets but keeps men centered in the public narrative.

An artist like Cardi, who brings via social media a mass audience with her, had less need to be built up or reliant on antiquated business models or standardized gatekeeping. After "Bodak Yellow" had swept the summer of 2017, *Pitchfork* critic Kristin Corry saw Cardi as the cultural shift she would become. Her essay titled "Why Cardi B's #1 Matters" expounds:

> Others have grazed the Hot 100 throne with No. 2s— Nicki Minaj with "Anaconda," Eve (and Gwen Stefani) with "Let Me Blow Ya Mind," Lil' Kim (and 50 Cent) with "Magic Stick"—but Cardi's chart dominance feels different.

[7]Ibid.

Though her rise is closely tied to her extremely candid social media approach, "Bodak Yellow" wasn't propelled by a specific meme. It doesn't make a play for pop listeners via cameos. And with Cardi being one of the very few female rappers to not play the role of the token woman in a respected rap crew, the immense mainstream success of "Bodak Yellow" could mark a turning point amid mounting frustration over Hip Hop's boys club … Cardi B suggests a new lane for female rappers—one that has little to do with seeking permission from male gatekeepers, pandering to white culture, or criticizing other women for their sexuality. It is about finding an audience on your own terms.[8]

One of the principle reasons men have forever feared matriarchies is because they believe women will rule in the same manner they have for thousands of years; when in fact societies helmed by women are frequently structured communally, have historically allowed for more sexual and economic freedom, and tend to have happier citizens.[9]

As an example of matriarchal power in Black art we can look to the world of film and director Ava DuVerny. *Variety* examined The OWN drama "Queen Sugar" noting it had

Made its mark on TV thanks to creator Ava DuVernay's decision to only hire women to direct the show, now in its seventh and final season. Variety spoke to all 42 directors (including DuVernay), who emphasized how

[8]https://pitchfork.com/thepitch/why-cardi-bs-bodak-yellow-no-1-matters/
[9]https://www.damemagazine.com/2013/05/10/five-things-we-know-about-societies-run-women/

her daring mandate changed the trajectory not only of their careers—with 39 of them getting their first episodic credit—but also of their lives.

Working on "Queen Sugar" had practical benefits: Many of the directors secured entry into the DGA, received health insurance and found representation for the first time. But the greatest gain may have been their newfound sense of confidence in their talents. That was a hard-won victory in an industry that has made it so hard, for so long, for women. Collectively, they refer to the changes brought about, thanks to the "Queen Sugar" initiative, as "the Ava Effect."[10]

Rap is slowly but surely becoming more matriarchal, in the most literal sense, as many Pussy Rappers are also mothers. Cardi herself had two children back to back after her major label debut.

Throughout the history of popular music women have given up children, forgone having them, and given up their careers to raise them. The number of mothers in the *Rock & Roll Hall of Fame* is shockingly low and the majority of those names compromised their career at some point to parent. Out of all the inductees, seemingly only Diana Ross and Madonna had children mid-career and were able to continue at their previous artistic output.

But now we have seemingly swung almost too far in the opposite direction.

---

[10]https://variety.com/lists/queen-sugar-42-women-directors-ava-duvernay/

Fans now expect artists to drop an album and a baby. Your reveal should be public. Pregnant artists performing to their literal due date happens with enough frequency that we compare them. Black women in modern America face staggering rates of both mother and infant mortality, making the stress of career and motherhood a life and death issue. Black women are also faced with super heroic expectations when it comes to careers and motherhood. Even the most celebrated and wealthy like Serena Williams, who most consider a superior human, have experienced frightening, traumatic deliveries, and stigmas regarding their return to work.

However, the upside is that pregnant bodies are normalized, even in various states of undress. As working women with children require childcare, which is mostly staffed by other women, space for nannies and kid-friendly backstages become part of touring norms and lean into the communal care style modeled in matriarchy.

The second matriarchal aspect to the ascension of Pussy Rap and Cardi as an artist is the sense of Femme Rap as a whole community. After years of being the "featured" girl, femme artists started collaborating with each other to create a new metric of success. Cardi has served as a model in encouraging other women to be part of the game and encouraging those women to do the same. By 2022, there were more femme collaborations than there had ever been in the history of the medium absolutely dominating the Top 40. When these women are in charge of their own labels and atop the power structure, we will see how Hip-Hop and matriarchy evolve.

As many femme and Pussy Rappers are comfortable with their bi and homosexuality, rapping with confidence that they really don't need a man for ANYTHING, there are a plethora of songs we can explore where male pleasure, desire, and feelings in general, are not at all part of the musical conversation.

Of course not everyone is on board. There are seemingly two schools. Those who subscribe to the theory "If one of us comes up, we all come up." And another who wants to feud.

It's probably not a coincidence that the latter have benefited most from the patriarchal system in place.

What we've seen in a post *Invasion of Privacy* world is that with a proliferation of women in the Rap game, many of whom have been lifted by their affiliation with her and their ability to dominate in all facets of commerce and culture, the "Cardi Effect" is real.

Lizzo and interviewer Zane Lowe reflected on Cardi's impact in an interview with Apple Music:

> ZL: I think it's important to recognize the relationship you and Cardi have on the record (the single "Rumors"). It's like an entire bar lined up with shots of "fuck you" juice.
>
> Lizzo: Cardi B to me is like the ultimate. She has always done it right. Everything she said, every way she has reacted, and that's because she did it being true to herself the whole time. She never did it to be cool, she never did it to be accepted or to be liked.
>
> ZL: She's a Ground breaker. You can't deny her ability.
>
> Lizzo: She is a fucking superstar and she has changed the game forever for a lot of us, you know, a lot of women. I

don't think she even realizes she is doing it because she is like, "I'm trying to just be successful, I'm trying to get this money. I want to live a happy life" and she just follows her heart. And that's why I love her.

There is something about women in power that the world just explodes for and I think woman haven't really been given, well … obviously, we've been marginalized, to a certain degree where we haven't been able to rise to that seat of power, again. And I'm going to say again, because we used to. And now we're back and we are coming back to our place in power and you can tell the difference.

She goes on to tell that as a woman in Indie Rap she was constantly questioned about what it was like "being a woman in rap, as if we were a minority in a huge sea of Penis Rap" but when asked what the future would hold for women she said:

I really think one day there is going to be so many girls that rap that you're not going to be able to keep up with them. We will fill a whole festival line up ourselves. Just like how there are so many dudes rapping and they all like got the same names, and they are sounding the same, a lot of them, and there is just so many you can't keep up, it's going to be the same with girls ….

There's just something about us. There were women rapping and there always have been and it feels like the floodgates are opening. I feel like where it was difficult to get through and you had to be exceptional or you had to have the right co-sign or you had to have help—now it's just like "Bitch, what's good?" A big butt and a smile? And I got eight bars? What's good? Let's Go![11]

*****

Whereas *Invasion of Privacy* began with a siren, it ends with an arresting rasp.

A disjointed, spooky music box creaks to the beat and SZA moans that she has nonchalantly left her man on "read," she is rocking YSL, she looks good, she is rich … and she does whatever the hell she likes. Her annunciation and delivery become more aggressive and she repeats the song's title.

A tinny, digital high-hat flutters in time and a blown out, but subtly mixed bass drum line by producers Murda Beatz and Cubeatz comes in and rides steady during the song. Cardi's cadence is almost militant and hearkens back to "Get Up Ten." It's her at her most assertive. She tells us about Bad Bitch divinity, bemoans broke hoes, shouts out designers, brags on her record setting musical accomplishments, and notes she's gotten more than Warhol ever bargained for in terms of her time in the public eye.

SZA pops back in with the chorus before Cardi lists her rules for being the baddest and instructions for keeping all the undistinguished gentlemen in her life in line. Be a lady, no thanks, she's got word play instead. She provocates that she does exactly what she likes, she spends and says what she

---

[11]Lizzo: "Rumors" with Cardi B, Delivering Hard Truths, and Manifesting Confidence | *Apple Music*.

wants, and you should only give it up if your man can make you richer.

SZA's chorus pops back in and gives you something to sing with. She plays with her vocals going in and out of her signature high notes against the eerie drone of the music box curdles back in bidding us adieu.

In a song full of quotable lines, it is in the earliest verse that she spits what could be the most memorable, and defining, lines on the album; one that will not only surmise the central thesis of *Invasion of Privacy* as a record, but more importantly the musical movement it will inspire. For years to come Rap femmes will offer us their take on the record's most potent summation:

"I'm a boss, I write my own name on the checks. Pussy so good I say my own name during sex."

The end.

After

Any music journalist considers themselves lucky to write a 33 1/3. That I was immersed in a genre that was establishing itself while I was enveloped in its music will be one of the greatest gifts of my career. From the time I began my proposal in the winter of 2021 and my deadline in March 2023, Pussy Rap, Femme Rap, and the femme presence in Hip-Hop has completely exploded. What I once sought out now populates numerous Spotify playlists with new femme artists and tracks being added rapidly. There are so many brilliant scholars of color doing work on the subject and as it evolves I hope there will be more.

On March 23, 2023, *NPR* released the second season of its groundbreaking podcast *Louder than a Riot.*[1] With titles like "Beauty is in the eye of the male gaze: DreamDoll, Doechii and Baby Tate," "What doesn't kill you makes you a strong Black woman: Rico Nasty," and "Baby girl, you're only funky as your last cut: MC Sha-Rock" their work details many of the topics

---

[1] https://www.npr.org/podcasts/510357/louder-than-a-riot

I've touched on with a depth, intimacy, and a formidable knowledge that is the very reason music journalism exists. Hosts Sidney Madden and Rodney Carmichael's work on the series and as independent journalists can't be overpraised. Their examination of the new wave of femme rapper and their struggles within the industry could be taught as a course.

In a rash decision, prior to the season airing, NPR cut *Louder than a Riot* from its programming schedule but allowed the final season to air. I'd encourage you to seek it out in any form you can, podcast or transcript, for as long as you can. It truly will go down as a golden archive of the era.

*****

One of the biggest challenges of writing about *Invasion of Privacy* is that unlike the vast majority of the 33 1/3 catalog, Cardi's debut not only still had a pulse, it was still running laps, breaking records, and making the news during my work. At the time of my acceptance Bloomsbury had never greenlit a record so young, but given its substantial impact, they agreed.

As of early June 2023 as I turn this in for the final time, the record and all of its tracks continue to populate the *Billboard* charts bumped by TikTok trends and the introduction of audio to Instagram.

In an anniversary piece marking the five years since the album's debut in April of 2023 *Complex* writer Peter A. Berry summarized *Invasion of Privacy*'s impact.

Much like Shea from *No Skips* he uses the "Victory Lap" as a marker of Cardi's success in a piece titled "Cardi B's Invasion of Privacy Is a Victory Lap That Continues to This Day."

Invasion of Privacy accomplished just about everything. Symbolically, it's a rare instance of the end result actually exceeding the hype in every way possible.

Every single song on the album charted on the Billboard Hot 100. Every track has been certified platinum or better. Invasion of Privacy won her the Grammy for Best Rap Album. In basketball terms, Cardi B's debut as a major label artist was like a first-year player winning Rookie of the Year, MVP, and a championship.

She made every shot she took. It was both an arrival and a takeover.[2]

Invasion of Privacy's long shelf life has also been extended due to the fact that as of June 2023 Cardi has yet to release her full length, follow up album, which has long been rumored to be titled *CB2.*

It has kept Vegas odds makers guessing as to when it will drop since 2020.

A pesky global pandemic and two kids in three years obviously impacted her ability to release a sophomore effort worthy of one of Rap's greatest debuts, not to mention get behind the media junket and global touring a record of that magnitude would require.

[2]https://www.complex.com/music/a/peter-a-berry/classics-cardi-b-invasion-of-privacy

But being Cardi she carved her own path.

From the top, she made it drop. Went up, up, up, till it stuck.

And built condos in our collective consciousness.

Queen Belcalis from the Bronx has proven she's here to rule, spinning her "lil'15 minutes" into five years and counting of nothing less than sheer cultural dominance.

Also Available

ALSO AVAILABLE

176. *Madonna's Erotica* by Michael Dango
177. *Body Count's Body Count* by Ben Apatoff
178. *k.d. lang's Ingénue* by Joanna McNaney Stein

179. *Little Richard's Here's Little Richard* by Jordan Bassett
180. *Cardi B's Invasion of Privacy* by Ma'Chell Duma